2023 Lucky Stars Horoscope

Stella Wilde

Copyright © 2023 by Stella Wilde

All rights reserved.

No portion of this book may be reproduced in any form or by any means without written permission from the publisher or author, except as permitted by U.S. copyright law.

The information provided within this book is for entertainment purposes only.

Even though the author has attempted to present accurate information, there are no representations or warranties, express or implied, about the completeness, accuracy, or reliability of the information contained in this book. The information is provided "as is," to be used at your own risk and discretion.

The methods described in this book represent the author's personal experiences. They are not intended to be a definitive set of instructions for this project. You may discover there are other methods and materials to accomplish this same end result and your results may differ.

Contents

Dedication	IV
1. How to Use This Book	1
2. 2023: The Year of Radical Regeneration	3
3. Jupiter Transits Aries: Daring Adventures	8
4. Saturn and Neptune in Pisces: Dream Bigger, Do Better	14
5. Uranus Unearths Gems from Unexpected Sources	23
6. Pluto Makes His Move Into Aquarius	29
7. Mercury Retrograde in Earth Signs	38
8. Jupiter Transits Taurus: Golden Opportunities	51
9. Nodal Shift: A New Door Opens to a New Destiny	57
10. Venus Retrograde in Leo: Questions Only the Heart Can Answer	64
11. Monthly Horoscopes and "Lucky Days"	70
12. Year Ahead Horoscope Summary & Affirmations	86
About Stella Wilde	93

For Derek & Julia

1

How to Use This Book

WHAT IS LUCK? IT'S often attributed to chance, fate, or destiny. You've had a lucky break, luck was with you (or not), fortune smiled upon you, etc. and so on.

I believe luck most often stems from *Awareness, Alignment, Action*, and *Alchemy*.

Awareness is based in using your life experience, personal values, and wisdom to inform your choices.

Alignment is based in using your intuition to decide if a certain thing feels right (and then listening to and acting upon what you've decided).

Action is based in taking responsibility for yourself, and doing what is necessary to create the outcome you desire.

Alchemy is based in the mysterious forces of the Universe, which include Universal Laws, Karma, and yes...Astrology.

Alchemy is a fancy word for "a seemingly magical process of transformation" (Oxford English Dictionary). When you are tuned into and tapped into astrological energies, you can use that Alchemy to enhance your own luck.

You can use astrological cycles and timings to schedule optimal times for having important meetings, starting creative projects, getting married, incorporating a business, launching a product or service, going on a trip, studying something new, etc. In whatever way you wish to transform your life, Astrology can help you.

When you're aware of astrological cycles, when you align with the energies, when you take action at more favorable times, you create an environment that supports alchemical magic. Often, synchronicities ensue. Doors open. Opportunities arrive.

As I say frequently on my YouTube channel, *it's all about using the energies, not letting them use you.*

To that end, I've done the hard work for you of figuring out how you can best use the astrology for 2023. I've provided an overview of the most significant (in my opinion) year ahead transits along with a much-requested feature: "lucky days" for each zodiac sign for each month. Please note that some of these "lucky days" may occur during retrograde periods. The world doesn't stop when planets retrograde. Just make sure to read the chapters in the book for advice on how to make the most of each astrological transit covered herein.

This book was written in the spirit of Jupiter, which is strong in my natal chart. Jupiter accentuates the positive, offers compassionate advice, and encourages personal growth. Within these pages, I hope you find the encouragement, guidance, and inspiration to manifest your wildest dreams in 2023. The stars are shining on you.

With love,

Stella

2

2023: The Year of Radical Regeneration

THE FIRST FEW WEEKS of 2023 may seem a little quiet, but don't let the temporary lull fool you. It's just a pause to regroup and re-commit yourself to taking action on the eye-opening epiphanies 2022 brought to your life. Overall, I proclaim 2023 as "The Year of Radical Regeneration," due to Saturn and Pluto shifting into new signs in March, and also a shift of the North Node into Aries in mid-summer. With Jupiter's ingress into Aries from December 20, 2022 to May 16, 2023, and the North Node also in Aries mid-July, there's a solid emphasis on renewal, rebirth, and regeneration. Aries is the promise of springtime, of life blooming again. And it will, my friends, it will.

But first we begin the year with a full moon in Cancer on January 6, with Mercury retrograde in Capricorn until January 19, and Mars also still retrograde in Gemini until January 12. We may feel a little emotionally "hung-over" from the prior year's intensity, and physical energy levels may not be at 100% peak performance. That's okay. Take time for some good old-fashioned self-care at the Cancer full moon and use the Mercury retrograde insights later on in this book to make the best use of this period.

The new year really kicks into gear after the new moon in Aquarius on January 21. The best time to take action on your goals is right after this through to April 20, when all planets will be in direct/forward motion. Without any retrogrades during that time, the energy is likely to flow more smoothly. Of course, you can make progress at other times of the year, but this golden period between January 21 and April 20th is especially favored because it also features several of the most beneficial aspects of the year, as follows:

March 3 - Venus conjuncts Jupiter in Aries

Wowza! This is big, feel good energy for taking risks in love and money, but with Jupiter's exuberance, do keep an eye on how far you're willing to go for romance and finances. The Law of Attraction is strongly in play with this transit, so keep your energy fire sign optimistic ("your vibe attracts your tribe"). Venus is acutely aware of aesthetics, and in Aries, she emphasizes well-groomed brows, red lipstick, and a devil-may-care attitude; conjunct Jupiter, she goes all out for her love interest (but be aware of the fine line between assertiveness and aggression). Sweetheart deals in business may come to fruition now, and it is a good time to seek a benefactor with "deep pockets." Venus conjunct Jupiter in Aries is favorable for a romantic getaway to somewhere warm where there's also a sense of adventure and excitement (think Las Vegas; Monte Carlo, Monaco; or Nassau, Bahamas).

Venus conjunct Jupiter in Aries has a touch of living *la vida loca* about it. And since this transit occurs during Pisces season, when the moon that day will be in Leo, the energy supports pursuing your dreams (Pisces) with flair (Leo). If I had to choose a day to get engaged, move in with someone, get married, start a business, or launch a product, this would be it. With the additional fiery Leo influence, grand gestures could go a long way toward sealing whatever deal in love and money you've got going on.

March 28 - Mercury conjuncts Jupiter in Aries

Say it with flowers, say it with heart, say it with chocolates, say it with a smile, or say it with a big ole diamond (Aries' birthstone is the diamond)—whatever—just say it. Write it. Market it. Teach it. Sing it. Poem it. Film it. Just get it out there into the world. Mercury in Aries tends to be a motormouth anyway, and Jupiter's expansiveness brings an added urgency to an already intense need to communicate. You could reach a wide audience with your wit and wisdom.

The moon's in Cancer during this transit, so be keenly aware of the emotional nuances of your words. Spontaneous improvisation on subject matters near and dear to your heart such as family, home, and self-care are favored—just be sure to consider the recipient of your message and how you can reach them with an enthusiasm that nurtures, but does not overwhelm. And be wary of appearing as a "know-it-all." Think inclusion rather than swaggering braggadocio when it comes to your communication style. A beneficial contract could be signed now, or you may book an important trip, news may arrive of a scholarship or award, an important client may sign up for your services, etc.

March 30 - Venus conjuncts Uranus in Taurus

A surprising win at the casino? A serendipitous meet-cute moment with someone who will become important in your life? A radical shift in your desires? Whatever ensues, you crave a wildly unique experience. Others may call you crazy—heck, you may call yourself crazy—as strange urges are stirred within you. Okay, maybe that's a bit over-dramatic, but in any case, the ordinary won't do. You fancy some big gesture, a sweep-you-off-your feet moment, and the Universe is primed to deliver it with this aspect.

Ruled by Venus, Taurus is all about luxury and sensuality—aesthetic experiences that are simply luscious. As the "Great Awakener," Uranus, when he encounters Venus, revivifies her, similar to the way a quenching rainstorm renews a parched field after a long drought. Your energetic field is tuned into the excitement of unusual possibilities to live your life like never before. Who knows what unconventional seeds will blossom from this astrological union, but they're sure to bring flowers with a heady scent that intoxicates. Allow yourself to live a little and explore a source of joy you perhaps would have never considered before this moment.

April 11 - Jupiter conjuncts the Sun in Aries

One of my favorite quotes is by the American novelist Henry James (also an Aries) who wrote, "Live all you can; it's a mistake not to." This is stellar advice for Jupiter conjunct the Sun in Aries. Some astrologers call this "the day of miracles" since Jupiter rules the ninth house of "God"/spirituality in the zodiac wheel, and when Jupiter conjuncts the Sun, fears are burned away in heaven's light and replaced with hope. Venus will slip into Gemini at 12:47 am eastern time and the moon will move into Capricorn at 1:33 pm eastern time (before that it will be void, which means, in brief, that nothing is likely to happen). So look to the afternoon for the best time to take advantage of this energy. The Sun in Aries exudes confidence and a can-do spirit; the moon that day in Capricorn highlights our ambitions; Venus in Gemini flirts with a couple of options; and Jupiter in Aries imbues an optimistic, exuberant feeling to expand your world.

Explore exciting possibilities for yourself that can take you to new heights—emotionally, spiritually, financially, creatively, etc. One of the dictionary definitions of the word "miracle" is "an outstanding example of something." Is your life an outstanding example of passionate fulfillment? What can you do to take charge of your life (Aries/Capricorn energy), be more open to various potentialities (Venus in Gemini), and live your truth (Jupiter in Aries)? Jupiter in Aries brings his good luck when we're taking the lead, inspiring others by our example, and going for our dreams with confidence and gusto.

Another quote that captures the feel of this transit is: "Don't quit before the miracle happens." The Aries and Capricorn vibe on this day emphasizes that unstoppable cardinal energy to initiate bold plans and see them through to fruition. So get back out there and get to it—and watch generous Jupiter lend a helping hand (in the form of money, resources, opportunity, connections, advice) to support your efforts to manifest a miracle in your world.

March and April are probably the two most important months of 2023, as Saturn leaves Aquarius for Pisces on the March 7, and Pluto makes his move into Aquarius on March 28. As planets near the end of their transit in a particular sign, there's often a final "release point" or "karmic wrap up" in the house where the planet is transiting in your natal chart. More on those Saturn and Pluto transits in separate chapters. In April we have a blockbuster Total Solar Eclipse, April 20, 2023, at 12:12 AM Eastern Time United States, at 29° Aries 50′. This eclipse is a preview of a longer chapter to come when the North Node shifts into Aries and transits there from July 18, 2023 to January 11, 2025. The new moon solar eclipse in April lights a fire in our hearts for new vistas. Even though Pluto is squaring the sun and moon, bringing a "how badly do you want it" vibe, you're willing to do the work because you sense that in some key area of your life, "it's now or never." More on this exciting solar eclipse in April's Monthly Lucky Stars chapter.

In 2023, you are re-aligning your life to the circumstances that have shifted for you since the Year of Radical Reinvention (which is what I called 2020 in my astrology book published then). With 2023's emphasis on all-things-new Aries, you will take on fresh challenges and opportunities that will reinvigorate your body, mind, and spirit—and that are uniquely suited to who you have become since 2020. It's about time, don't you think? I do, and I can't wait.

3

Jupiter Transits Aries: Daring Adventures

JUPITER RE-ENTERED ARIES ON December 20, 2022, and he will brazenly blow through the sign until May 16, 2023, throwing sparks as he goes. Jupiter's raison d'être is to help you *expand beyond your current reality, and to do so with enthusiasm and joy.*

Ruler of fire sign Sagittarius, Jupiter loves the simpatico vibe of fellow fire sign Aries, who's always eager for the next escapade. With Jupiter transiting Aries, you're encouraged to boldly and bravely set out on some new adventure like the Fool in the Tarot, taking a leap of faith and a chance on yourself. As American blind and deaf educator, author, and lecturer Helen Keller proclaimed, "Life is either a daring adventure or nothing at all." (And, interestingly enough, Keller was born with her natal Jupiter in Aries! In true Aries fashion, she was the first deaf-blind person to receive a college degree in 1904 [Aries is the pioneer and loves to be "first" in whatever they do]).

These "daring adventures" in the first half of 2023 may have a similar vibe to whatever was going on in your life from May 10, 2022 to July 28, 2022, when Jupiter was direct in Aries. Also, if a situation didn't fully deliver on its promise during that time frame, then the Universe is likely to bring something better now; Jupiter is certainly Generous (with a capital G) and can bring us second chances. Interestingly, Jupiter will conjunct Chiron the Wounded Healer in Aries on March 12, 2023, and whatever life wisdom you gleaned from May to July 2022 can be put into good practice. Chiron in Aries (natally and by transit) can often bring spiritual growth lessons when it comes to standing up for yourself, doing your own thing, and being the brave hero or heroine of your life. Overall, I think this is very positive energy that reinforces how far you've come on your healing journey, and that you are ready to confidently go forth and see where opportunity leads you.

Here's how you can bring the best benefit to yourself when Jupiter transits Aries:

ARIES: A lot has gone down since the last time Jupiter was in Aries in 2010…you've had Uranus transiting through your sign for seven long years, radically turning your life upside down; Pluto squaring your Sun, making you question your life choices; and then Chiron in Aries nudging you to put the finishing touches on karmic assignments you've been given in this lifetime. Sheesh! So I don't blame you if all this Jupiter in Aries hoopla is leaving you a little…*verklempt* (a Yiddish word meaning 'overcome with emotion' to the point of being choked up with tears). But let these be tears of joy, dear Ram. Everything is changing for the better; believe it. Believe in yourself again. I know it may be hard to take a chance on Life after the aforementioned astrological transits had their way with you, but that's exactly what will bring you good fortune now: a reconnection with your sunny, can-do, move-mountains optimism and your hard-headed Rammy determination to be the best at whatever is important to you. Jupiter's daring adventure is to thrust you upon the center stage of Life again, in the spotlight, the star of the show. Are you ready for your close-up? I assure you: this is no opening night box office flop, but the beginning of a very exciting, lucrative, and happy second act of your story.

TAURUS: Unseen hands are pulling strings behind the scenes, making sure you're in the right place at the right time. Divine appointments abound, perhaps with an important teacher or healer that gifts you profound insight. Your daring adventure is to align with the unequivocal "yes" that comes from deep inside you, and that is perfectly in tune with the spiritual workings of the Universe to the point where you trust the directives even though you can't explain exactly why. You just *know*.

GEMINI: Jupiter transiting through your house of hopes and wishes invites a genie in a bottle into your life, Gemini— granting you three wishes. Use them wisely. I would never tell you what to wish for, but I will say this: perhaps wish for daring new adventures in the emotional, intellectual, and spiritual realms. And consider allowing one of the wishes to not only benefit you, but to make the world a better place as well. You see in real time that what goes around, comes around—and your own good karma for past charitable deeds returns to you tenfold.

CANCER: At the zenith of your chart, Jupiter in Aries promises career kudos, opportunities, and rewards if you've earned them. You could reach an amazing career milestone now that leads to a promotion, a new career direction, or even a lucrative retirement (depending on your personal situation). The daring adventure that Jupiter brings is also an affirmation of what you are capable of—a sort of prelude for what's to come with the North Node transit of Aries that begins in July. Travel for professional reasons can be favorable now, and may be the catalyst for an important introduction that leads to career change with the North Node transit.

LEO: Jupiter in fellow fire sign Aries brings you the passion to embrace the world with your arms wide open, face turned to the sunshine, a warm breeze caressing your skin. Travel to a warmer climate may be just the thing you need to shake off the winter blues. But even if you choose to stay home, you still want to connect with the world—and Jupiter supports online endeavors such as teaching and learning—and writing, marketing, publicity projects that could ensure you reach a wide audience. You are able to take the pulse of future trends and be ahead of the curve in some way that benefits you. Additionally, improvements in relationships with your in-laws are possible now—a trip to see them or a trip you all go on together can be a healing balm if there have been any family tensions.

VIRGO: Angels come in all shapes and sizes, both in the flesh and in the spirit. An "angel investor" could show up, suffusing time, money, and energy into your life—with tangible results you may be able to literally take to the bank. You may also have a strong connection with angels on the other side, who are guiding you to exactly the resources you need to launch yourself on a path of daring achievement. One of these resources is greater self-confidence and belief that what you want is possible. It is.

LIBRA: As the occupier of the seventh house of relationships, and ruled by Venus, you are here to teach the rest of us all about love and connection—so it is a sad state of affairs indeed when Libra is Lonely (and yes, it needs to be capitalized because it is that much of a big deal for you!). Whether that Loneliness stems from the lack of a partner, a BFF who really gets you, or a business colleague who's on your side, be of good cheer, Libra, because Jupiter is about to offer you daring new adventures with Significant Someones. Your best chances for easing this Loneliness and meeting Someone who could become Significant in your life once the North Node moves into Aries mid-July is through travel, educational environments (community college class or book club, anyone?), spiritual groups, and the gym. Get out there and flash them that gorgeous Libra smile—which melts hearts, doesn't it, darling?

SCORPIO: *Health is wealth*, and Jupiter transiting your sixth house of work and well-being reminds you of this important axiom. Your daring adventure with this transit is to make sure your life is in balance, so that wealth continues to accrue through work, but not at the expense of your health. Can you schedule in a short trip, not for work, but to rest and rejuvenate? If your daily life could benefit from better health routines, Jupiter can help you find an exercise regimen that you enjoy—maybe something that's a little adventurous, such as jujitsu, boxing, or fencing (but of course check with a doctor before doing so). Jupiter encourages you to take greater responsibility for your own well-being—and you could benefit from educating yourself on nutrition, treatments, modalities, etc. and then committing to what you feel is right for you. Jupiter could also bring a favorable change to your work environment, such as a new boss (who's a vast improvement over the previous one), new hires to your department who actually know what they're doing, and the possible removal (via the Universe) of some co-worker thorn in your side.

SAGITTARIUS: Like Shakespeare, you could be penning sonnets about someone in your world who is *more lovely and temperate than a summer's day*...someone with whom there is *a marriage of true minds*...someone who is *a fair friend who can never be old*. Whether Jupiter rejuvenates a love relationship of long-standing or brings someone new into your life, you will be rapping or rhapsodizing in lyrical terms. And that's the thing that could be the most daring adventure of all: putting the songs of your heart into creative form—whether you're writing books, songs, poems or making babies—love expands your world in myriad ways. Enjoy!

CAPRICORN: Add on an "h" to "heart" and you get "hearth," the source of fire in homes built of yore. I'm here to remind you that the heart is like a hearth, isn't it—a center of fiery passion that causes us to follow our dreams, fall in love, and travel the world. Pluto's transit in your sign may have made you feel like your heart fire went out, but I assure you, Jupiter's coming to embolden your spirit and ignite the guttering flame with some Jupiterian natural gas. Your daring adventure may manifest as discovering or reconnecting with parts of yourself that may have been abandoned long ago in order to satisfy family and/or society obligations. Use Jupiter's energy to free your soul through travel, spiritual studies, improvements to your home to make it more *you*—including a re-do of your home office (what Capricorn doesn't have a home office?). And for those of you who've outgrown where you're living, it's time to find the place that is more aligned with the direction you see yourself headed in—away from the hearth where you were born and raised.

AQUARIUS: This transit can give you immense knowledge and personal fulfillment in writing, speaking, teaching, networking, sales—if only you would focus for five minutes. There's so many exciting projects and possibilities, and only so many hours in the day. You learned with Saturn's recent transit through your sign to take your time and discern that which is most important to you. So use Saturn's wisdom to temper Jupiter's tendency to do more, be more, say more, consume more, etc. Jupiter could lead you to discover surprising ways to use your intellect—and you could become a trail-blazer with some sort of technique, invention, or product. Jupiter through your third house helps you massively tune into the Law of Attraction, and you can manifest miraculous improvements in your daily life.

PISCES: More money means more choices, and Jupiter could be bringing more of both of those into your life as it bankrolls your second house with enough wherewithal to make a few dreams come true. But here's the thing: Saturn is also in your sign as of March 7, encouraging you to use your discernment when it comes to managing your life—and that includes your resources. So, do not let any bounty slip through your fingers via impulsive purchases, crazy schemes, or "lending" to needy friends who only show up when you're flush. Have a system in place (very Saturn) to "pay yourself first" via a savings or investment account—and then you can party like it's 1999. In fact, Jupiter was retrograde in Aries from October 23, 1999, to February 14, 2000. As Jupiter likes to bring second chances, it's perfectly possible that something from that time period comes round again in another, better form—or that something you invested in then benefits you now (like if you started/changed careers or got a degree, investing in yourself, which pays off handsomely through some serious coinage).

4

Saturn and Neptune in Pisces: Dream Bigger, Do Better

ON MARCH 7, SATURN enters Pisces, where it has not been since April 7, 1996. It takes Saturn 29 and a half years to make its way around the astrological wheel. Saturn is slow, determined, focused; he is the Lord of Time, the Supervisor of Rules and Restrictions, the Kahuna of Karmic Responsibility. His energy can be heavy, dour, basic. Ruler of Capricorn (and ancient ruler of Aquarius [whose ruler became Uranus after it was discovered in 1781]), Saturn is an iron hand in a scratchy wool glove—no cushy velvet for him. No pain, no gain—but the rewards can be worth it in the end if you keep your promises, work hard, and fulfill your obligations.

Saturn is not totally heartless; he just wants to see that you mean business—because he certainly does. So he will test you. A Saturn transit can feel like you're Hercules tasked with 12 impossible labors—and just when you think you're done—along comes another task. Eventually, if you keep plodding along patiently, doing your best, staying true to your word, the skies will clear and voilà! You have weathered the Saturnian storm.

All the planets have their pluses and minuses, and Saturn is no exception. We need Saturn to bring structure to life, to give us a framework of rules and standards to live by, to provide the discipline to get a job done. How would we know what achievement looked like if we didn't have criteria by which to measure our results?

Ah, but ruled by Neptune, Pisces measures success differently. Compassionate creatures, flexible, adaptable, Pisces knows there is no "one size fits all" way to approach the world; there are many paths to the same destination, and they would prefer to bend the "Saturn rules" as they go—or ignore them completely. Saturn contains; Neptune flows. So you see the potential discomfort Saturn may encounter in Pisces.

Even so, we can actually use Saturn in Pisces to great advantage. It's interesting that Neptune, Pisces' ruler, is also in Pisces now, and it has entered the Scorpio decan (the last ten degrees of Pisces) where transformation becomes a highly intuitive and transcendentally spiritual experience. Saturn is quivering in his jackboots; he knows he has his work cut out for him to try and rule the unruly—Neptune will just shape shift and disappear in an etheric mist, leaving Saturn fuming because Saturn *hates* to feel ineffective.

So how to reconcile these two energies? Let me tune into my past life as a college English professor and give you an example (which I am simplifying somewhat for brevity's sake). When writing poetry, you can choose a closed or open form for your lines. Open form means you shape the length of the lines and stanzas on the page however you would like—there are no rules, only the rules that your creativity decides upon. In closed form poetry, you must adhere to the standard, agreed-upon form of the poem you have chosen. For example, if you decide to write a sonnet, that sonnet must be 14 lines, and it needs to follow a certain rhyme scheme. (There are many other types of closed form poems—villanelles, sestinas, ballads, limericks—just to name a few—all with their own distinct "rules.")

Poetry rises up from the depths of dreams, the subconscious, and the misty interplay between your Muse and your Imagination; poems are a Neptunian art form. When you write a closed form poem, you use the "rules" of Saturn as a structural template for the ethereal. Having to follow a rhyme scheme and pre-determined line length can actually act as a stimulant to get your brain to come up with even a more creative vision than the one you originally started with. In this way, Saturn and Neptune can help you *dream bigger, and do better.*

> *Saturn in Pisces can help you do the work to manifest the dream that could change your life.*

But your tendency to procrastinate will be tested; you may have to give up your escapist binge-watching of Netflix rom-coms (*Emily in Paris*, anyone?); you will need to pull yourself up by your purple Pisces bootstraps and make no excuses—because Saturn has no time for those. You must show up and "become your dream" and do the damn work. You ready?

You will need:

- A transformative vision for your life that plays out like a movie in your daydreams.

- A non-negotiable slot of time every day, every other day, once a week—whatever—during which you devote yourself to actually take concrete steps toward your goal. Over time, these incremental actions will add up to accomplishment; you're in this for the long haul.

- A way to hold yourself accountable to getting the work done (coach, mentor, group "mastermind" etc.).

- Small rewards for doing the work that motivate you to keep going.

- The ability to draw proper boundaries around your time so that you make yourself a priority. Saturn can help you set limits with others by teaching you how to say "no."

Viewed through this interpretive lens, you can use the Saturn in Pisces transit as follows:

ARIES: Saturn will move through your twelfth house; your subconscious may be stirring up all sorts of urgency regarding the passage of time and all the items on your "bucket list" you still haven't completed. You're pondering what you still want to accomplish in your life, your legacy, the ways you've supported yourself, the ways you've sometimes been your own worst enemy. This transit helps you carefully go through a soul retrospection wherein you can realistically sift through when you've sacrificed, what you've achieved, and times you've loved and lost. Aries doesn't usually enjoy this type of introspection (unless maybe you have a Scorpio or Capricorn Moon or Ascendant), but I suggest you don't avoid it. As the North Node is also in your sign during the Saturn in Pisces transit, directing you to a new destiny, you want to make sure you are headed in the right direction. And how will you know if you do not examine your deepest motivations?

TAURUS: Saturn will bring you the structured discipline to manifest one of your wildest dreams during his transit of your eleventh house. And while you have legendary patience, Uranus in your sign and then Jupiter (from mid-May 2023 to mid-year 2024) is making you perhaps a bit impatient: you want results *now*. Saturn doesn't deal in shortcuts, however. Plus as you continue to go through Uranus's electrifying personal upheaval, what you want may change (and abruptly so). Therefore, I suggest that instead of focusing on what the dream *looks* like, you focus instead on what the dream *feels* like. Be responsible (Saturn) and provide yourself with whatever you need to bring that emotion into your life, and then the external reality will adjust itself nicely. For example, if you want to manifest a new love relationship, do what you can now to make yourself feel loved: surround yourself with caring friends, treat yourself with kindness, etc., instead of obsessively chasing after a certain person or stalking dating apps in search of the "one." Take care of your own side of things, and the Universe will do the rest in its own good time.

GEMINI: Saturn is making sure that your star rises high in the sky; whenever Saturn is at the peak of your chart in the tenth house of career, you will surely be in high demand. But "high demand" also means more work, more responsibility, more "eyes" on you. You are coming into one of the most fruitful times in your life for achieving your career goals; promotions, kudos, recognition and reward can all be yours—but this is no time to shirk. Saturn still expects you to work for these blessings. You would be well advised to improve your organizational and time-management skills and put systems into place that help you manage mundane tasks (because you simply will not have time to attend to them). Can you do your grocery shopping online? Invest in a housekeeper once a month? Use online tools and phone apps to keep your schedule on track so that you don't miss important meetings? If you have to spend a little money to support the infrastructure of your life in these ways, it is money well-invested.

CANCER: Saturn wants you to think seriously about your future. You feel a yearning for a richer understanding of Life and your place in it, and what you can do to actualize your gifts in the world. You may benefit from a "spiritual retreat" in order to reconsider your commitments. The key with this transit is to discipline your mind and not let it trick you into defeatist thinking. You could be working toward some significant achievement—such as attaining a credential/college degree, writing a book-length manuscript, or building an online business. The investment of time will be worth it; don't let yourself be derailed by distractions/shiny object syndrome. Stick to the "one true thing" and believe in yourself to get the job done.

LEO: Saturn brings his *gravitas* to an already heavy house—the eighth—where we must deal with the more "weighty" aspects of life:

sex, death, healing, physical intimacy, other people's money, the taboo, and psychic experiences. The eighth house involves other people and their resources—what they bring into our lives—for better or worse. So with Saturn transiting here, you are being very pragmatic in this regard. Do people add to your life in a positive sense, or do they lurk over you like a dark cloud, dimming your natural Leo sunshine? Saturn energy relates to structure and boundaries—and you may tasked with creating both in your life. While you must not avoid your responsibilities to others, there is also a limit. You have little patience for superficiality during this transit, as you may keenly feel the passage of time, and recognize the importance of making the most of every day you have.

VIRGO: Saturn in your seventh house of partnerships (both business and personal) puts your commitments to the test. Are you in or are you out? Well, it all depends. You want serious connections now with responsible people, and if they can bring the level of maturity you require, then great. If not, you may agonize for a while until you finally pull the plug and end it. If you meet someone new during this transit who's a "keeper," there could be some obstacle/delay in getting together—perhaps their divorce is pending, or they live a distance from you, or they travel a lot for work, etc. Saturn usually brings tests, so don't let this deter you if the commitment is mutual. You can make it work if you're both invested—and if you meet each other halfway. In any case, do not rush into any serious commitments; Saturn advises to take it slow. In terms of business, a well-respected mentor may enter your life during this transit; whatever they teach you could help you save a lot of time in the long run.

LIBRA: Saturn will demand that you get serious about your work and well-being. If you've been slacking in sticking to a healthy diet and fitness regime, Saturn is going to pressure you to get yourself together in that regard. An ounce of prevention is worth a pound of cure, Saturn advises, so better to change your diet now and lose ten pounds while you only have ten to lose than ignore the situation and gain thirty more pounds—making it even more difficult to shift the weight. In terms of your job, you may be working longer hours and taking on more responsibility. If the situation becomes too onerous, you may decide to quit; however, Saturn advises that you have a back up plan before you up and leave. Wherever Saturn is transiting in our charts, he forces us to be held accountable. And Saturn can teach us some hard lessons when we try to take shortcuts or avoid doing the right thing. Do your best to support yourself with a schedule that helps you maintain or improve your health despite the demands of your job—and that includes finding time for proper rest.

SCORPIO: Saturn encourages you to commit to your creative life force energy and build something from your talents. Neptune transiting through this fifth house has stirred your imagination for the last several years, but dreaming is not enough—and you will feel that sense of urgency now to manifest your creative dreams into concrete form. Come up with a viable / sustainable schedule for yourself that includes built-in time periods for your creative pursuits. Saturn reminds us that *good things take time*. If you apply yourself regularly, you can have something substantial to show for your efforts by the end of Saturn's transit. Do not let doubt stop you—or the demands and distractions of others. The fifth house also rules "pleasure"—and if you want a significant achievement, you may have to delay your gratification until the project is complete. But Saturn promises that the reward will be worth the sacrifice in the end—and besides, if the creative act brings you joy, then it's the best kind of work in the world—and even dour old taskmaster Saturn can get on board with that.

SAGITTARIUS: Saturn in your fourth house of home, family, and roots brings attention to how secure you feel in the world—the literal security of your home and your family's safety—and your inner feelings of knowing you can take care of yourself, that you have everything you need. It's time to get serious about the foundation of your life and fix whatever is broken (and with Neptune in this house, you could be dealing with a need to fix wells, pipes, water heaters, etc.). Also, you may need to be the "bigger person" to mend fences with a family member. It's time to clean up your life, so decluttering is advised. Sometimes this transit can bring about a move due to a job relocation. You may be dealing with emotional ups and downs and trying to get a handle on them; try not to give into Neptune's propensity for escapism. Instead, clean out a drawer, organize your pantry, or do laundry—something productive that also supports your daily well-being.

CAPRICORN: Saturn moving through your third house of the mind, communication, daily life/environment brings a "reality check" to these areas. For example, is there chaos all around you with stacks of papers, unfinished projects, snack wrappers (because you eat at your desk all the time)? Do you suffer from negative self-talk? Do you tend to lower your expectations as a sort of defense mechanism? Have you even thought about these things/noticed them (probably not because you're too busy building your empire—let's be honest). Saturn in your third house would like you to consider how you can consciously create a more healthy atmosphere by paying more attention to what you literally say to yourself and what your environment says about your state of mind/being—and then clean up your act. Also ponder this: do you sacrifice your originality in favor of achievement and the "security" of approval? The third house is about learning: during this transit, you're in the School of Capricorn, as Saturn is your ruling planet. The curriculum contains lessons in leaving behind bad habits, learning more about who you really are, and communicating with greater authenticity.

AQUARIUS: Saturn makes his move into your second house of money and values, stirring your desire to get your financial house in order. You've just spent the last three years during Saturn's transit of your first house re-examining your priorities and making some difficult decisions about your life direction. Now you're ready to manifest the resources you need to put those new plans and commitments into motion. With Saturn, there are no quick fixes, so forget any get-rich-quick schemes. Instead, go old-school and get back to the basics: regular, automatic deposits from your paycheck into a savings account; a part-time gig (in addition to your full-time job) to pay down debt; the "envelope system" of budgeting (google it). Because results often don't come quickly with Saturn, we can get impatient and then give up, so find a way to track even incremental progress toward your financial goals so that you see your results (however modest) in black and white. Saturn transiting your second house encourages you to get serious about your value and worth. Is it time to raise your prices if you own your own business? Is it time to ask for a raise from your employer? Address areas where you shortchange yourself, and don't settle for less.

PISCES: Saturn transiting your first house of the Self has its positives—although at times his energy may make you feel like a Victorian Lady whose circulation is being cut off by a too-tight corset: you simply can't draw a deep enough breath. But Saturn only pulls the strings too tight when he needs to remind you to rein in your daydreaming, darling, and pay attention to your body. If you've been in denial about some aspect of your physical well-being, Saturn may bring some harsh truths home, but he can also help you establish better health habits. Saturn encourages you to slim down your life—literally, figuratively. It's time to give up empty calories, empty relationships, empty bank accounts. Others may not understand why you're so serious all of a sudden—and you might not even understand it entirely yourself, either. Structure and routine can lead to personal breakthroughs—if you can stay disciplined and work your Pisces 2.0 Program, which includes maintaining proper boundaries so that others cannot dissuade you from your goals. One day during this transit you'll start seeing the shift: a few pounds gone, a few false friends vanished, and a few more dollars in your bank account—and you will finally be able to breathe again.

5

Uranus Unearths Gems from Unexpected Sources

IN 2023, WE'RE RIGHT at the midpoint of Uranus's seven-year transit through Taurus. Those born from May 6 to May 14 are dealing this year with Uranus conjunct their Sun, revolutionizing their identities, radically changing their goals, and upending situations long in need of a reboot. Uranus is wild-card energy; he's the planet of revolutions, revelations, reinvention, eccentrics, excitement, technology, astrology, science, inventions, the future. Uranus's essence has the quality of a pulsating electrical current…with occasional power surges. When the planet is going direct (from January 22 to August 28), Uranus is more likely to blow a few fuses just to remind everybody he's the father of electricity, the god of lightning, wind, and awakenings that propel us into a future that we think we're not always ready for (but actually, we are).

While he's been in Taurus, Uranus has been rocking through the crust and the mantle right down to the core of your life, bringing to the surface every issue you may have about money, safety and security needs, and living by your values. Once Uranus has delivered his news on blast, it's hard to stay in any sort of cognitive dissonance. I mean you can, of course, stay in denial, but Uranus often delivers his message multiple times until you take it seriously and make the change.

Now that we're halfway through his transit through earthy Taurus, you are perhaps a bit more used to how Uranus has been impacting you, but you certainly don't want to get complacent. You just never know with Uranus and his shenanigans. A sign known to love its familiar routines, Taurus (in all fairness) can benefit from a Uranian shake-up every now and again. Wherever you have Taurus in your natal chart, it's often easier to skate along on the surface of life without looking too deeply or asking too many questions; you just want to keep things *comfortable*. Often it takes a Uranian transit to prompt a deep soul searching and propel you out of said comfort zone. And it is exactly that Uranian lightning-bolt situation that unearths truths that you've been hiding even from yourself, revelations that require you to take action. As the poet Rumi wrote, "Let us carve gems out of our stony hearts and let them light our path to love."

When Uranus is direct from January 22 until August 28, his exclamatory and exuberant energy may more directly impact your life, but at least we are not dealing with the Saturn/Uranus square this year as we did in 2022. That transit caused grinding frustration and tension for months over situations that seemed at a dead-end stalemate until they finally and dramatically shifted during the final eclipses in 2022.

In fact, when Uranus met up with the North Node in Taurus July/August/September of 2022, you may have been redirected suddenly and surprisingly from a path, circumstance, or relationship you thought was solid and secure, only to have Uranus deliver one more surprise up his sleeve during the October and November 2022 eclipses. In 2023, you may clearly see why those redirections were necessary, especially around the full moon lunar eclipse in Scorpio on May 5, 2023, when the Sun and Uranus will be conjunct in Taurus and Mercury will be retrograde in Taurus. A Uranian-induced epiphany may help you put into perspective whatever happened in 2022, and, in some cases, show you the blessing in disguise.

Uranus is often involved when it comes to sudden strokes of good luck, downloads of genius ideas, and being in the right place at the right time.

Here's how to benefit from Uranian influence in 2023:

ARIES: Continue to ride the wave of Uranus's unpredictable transit of your money house. If you come into some unexpected funds, manage this boon wisely: pay off debts, save some, and treat yourself to a modest goodie. Your own genius is the best resource for earning extra cash at this time. Monetize your brain by investing your time into writing a book, teaching a course, inventing a new product or service—and then get it out there in the world, especially after the north node enters your sign in mid-July.

TAURUS: Continue the process of radically re-inventing yourself. Keep going with the Great Purge, getting rid of the old and outmoded junk from your life: clothes that don't reflect who you're evolving into; routines that keep you stuck in boring obligations; connections that don't get the "new you" (and may even have disdain for the direction your life is heading). Hey, it's your life and you can do what you want! Tap into that Uranian rebellious streak and with Jupiter in your sign from mid-May onward, dare yourself to travel beyond all pre-conceived notions you've ever had of yourself and what you are capable of.

GEMINI: Continue to benefit from flashes of lightning bolt brilliance and inspiration that Uranus has favored you with over the last few years. In many ways, his transit of your twelfth house of the subconscious is like the trailer of a movie you'll be living after 2025 when Uranus enters your sign and further amplifies your genius. With warp speed, you can rid yourself of limiting beliefs and self-sabotaging behaviors. Pay attention to when/how Uranus flips a switch, instantaneously releasing the mental, emotional, and spiritual hold certain dramas have had over you. You're free.

CANCER: Continue to collect an assortment of new friends whose eccentric flair inspires you to bring your own genius out of its shell a bit more than you usually do. Say yes to spontaneous invitations, especially to take a class/learn something new and/or travel when Uranus is moving forward in the sky. It's time to put yourself out there by connecting with a wider variety of personal and professional organizations—and the more "niche," the better (like the Sea Glass and Sand Dollar Beachcombers Club who meet every Saturday at the local beach, searching for treasures). You will find riches in places you have never looked before.

LEO: Continue to ride the rollercoaster of change that Uranus has brought to your career. It may be advisable to uplevel your skills when it comes to technology so that you improve your chances in a demanding job market. You may finally find that 2023 is the year you break free from a limiting career circumstance and either get the promotion you deserve (even if it means moving on from your current employer), start your own business, or retire. After the north node enters Aries, you may yearn to live the laptop lifestyle and travel and/or work abroad for an international company. You want more recognition in the world, and you are willing to make the necessary changes in order to get it. Don't let anyone make you feel bad or guilty for wanting to shine.

VIRGO: Continue to envision greatness for your life and how you can expand your world through traveling internationally, writing a book, going to graduate school, etc. You've already had several epiphanies that have shaken you down to the roots, showing you where and how you perhaps hold yourself back. You're ready now to take some surprising leaps of faith and explore new literal and spiritual territory. You're braver than you give yourself credit for.

LIBRA: Continue to process through the psychological, spiritual, and emotional awakening Uranus has conjured in your life the last several years. He's not done with you yet, but now the epiphanies are a little less jarring. You're reconnecting with parts of yourself that you've been unwilling to face for quite a while—perhaps even lifetimes. You're bringing up gems of insights from rich soil, and you can use these to inspire your artistry and serve as inspiration for others.

SCORPIO: Continue to evolve through the shake-ups in your personal relationships as Uranus transits your seventh house of relationships. The North Node will be in Taurus your seventh house until mid-July 2023. While Jupiter is also in Taurus beginning mid-May, you will have three powerhouse energies helping you meet someone special (whether in a business and/or personal sense). Make the most of getting out and about from May 16 to July 16 and see who the Universe brings across your path. You could be surprised by a spoonful of sugar in the most delightful way.

SAGITTARIUS: Continue to take inspired action on finding a better balance between work and personal life so that you have time to take care of your well-being (go to the gym, attend health appointments, relax regularly, etc.). Ascertain whether you are living to work or working to live and adjust accordingly. Learn some new technology that may improve your skills in the workplace and help you stabilize your finances. Living your life authentically is imperative—try not to compromise what matters most to you concerning your well-being.

CAPRICORN: Continue to explore your options when it comes to what brings you delight, Capricorn. Uranus could suddenly surprise you with quirky creative ideas, connections with lovable eccentrics, and spontaneous pleasures (quickie weekend away, anyone?). An innovative technology could be the key to unlocking greater prosperity for you this year. See how you can use it in your work and/or in promoting yourself. Your love life is due for a radical regeneration, that's for sure. Between mid-May and mid-July, someone new may enter the scene or, if you're already involved, you may put a ring on it.

AQUARIUS: Continue to take care of the foundation of your life as Uranus is known to bring abrupt shifts to home and family when he barrels through your fourth house. You may suddenly buy or sell property; someone may spontaneously move in or move out; you may radically alter your way of life through downsizing or upsizing (due to a new baby in the family or a relative needing to move in with you). With Saturn going through your sign and squaring your ruling planet Uranus in 2022, you could have felt a disconnect between self and habitat and an overwhelming desire for a geographical cure to start your life over in a place that aligns more with your energy. This could be your year to find your place in the sun.

PISCES: Continue to ride with the changes Uranus has brought to your daily life, as the cosmos encourages greater independence and control over your own schedule. Your mind has been percolating with all sorts of genius inspirations, and now with Saturn in your sign as of early March, you have the discipline to put these visions into some sort of concrete form. Use technology and organizational tools to create systems that save you time so that there's more energy and head space for your projects. This year you could suddenly find yourself thrust in front of a local group to share your talents and expand your social circle.

6

Pluto Makes His Move Into Aquarius

FIND A CAPRICORN AND ask them to tell you a story about the good old days, and they'll have to go far back into the archives pre-2008, before Pluto entered their sign. Every Capricorn is sure to have at least one hair-raising story about "bulldozer of doom" Pluto's mud-slinging, ass-kicking demolition of their world.

But there's another analogy that is fitting for Pluto: that of a cosmic midwife, shepherding you through the processing of birthing a new and better reality into your life. Sure, it's likely to hurt (birth is a messy, painful process), but Pluto's there to coach you to dig deep into your soul to push harder, you're almost there.

To be sure, the beginning of a Pluto transit is hard: he comes in like a wrecking ball, bulldozer, battle ax and you wonder what the living F has hit you…but what is going to bloom in Pluto's volcanic ash soil *requires* the flat-lined, scorched earth of what feels like doom (and can manifest, to be sure, in dramatically intense circumstances, losses, betrayals, desolations, challenges, etc.)—again, just ask any Capricorn.

Even so, one of the things that's wonderful about astrology is that you can see when cycles are due to shift—you just have to hold on, do the work the transit is requiring of you as best you can—and keep the faith.

Every planet promises a result. Pluto promises to not abandon you in the end, but to be there by your side to midwife you through what may have been a very scary ride through the new life birth canal.

Pluto will make his move into Aquarius from March 23, 2023 to June 11, 2023. Then he'll retreat into Capricorn to ensure he's done all he set out to do in that sign. From January 20, 2024, until September 1, 2024, he's back in Aquarius; and then from September 1 to November 19, he'll retrograde for the final time into Capricorn. From November 19, 2024 onward until March 8, 2043, he will be in Aquarius "for good" — until he enters Pisces in 2043.

Pluto in Aquarius brings to the forefront issues that involve the collective, technology, astrology, space flight/aliens, freedom, genius, surprising events, and the future.

> Pluto's transit through Aquarius encourages all of us to question: *what does it mean to be human?*

As the ruler of the eighth house underworld, Pluto is intimately familiar with Soul—and your Soul's deepest urges to "only connect"—with your creativity, your sexual nature, your intuitive capabilities, your psychology, your purpose, and your karma. Believe what you will about where the Soul comes from—or where it goes after physical death—but ultimately, many of us can agree that there is a "Spirit" within each of us that makes us alive—and which connects us to the Divine. Perhaps Ralph Waldo Emerson explains it best: "...within man, is the soul of the whole; the wise silence; the universal beauty to which every part and particle is equally related; the eternal One."

Pluto's transit through Aquarius will likely bring situations that challenge us to preserve our humanity. *Questions to think about:* Do you want a chip implanted in your body to track your every move, purchase, and thought? Do you want Artificial Intelligence to replace human artistry and create art, writing, music that may be pleasant, but that is unlikely to move you emotionally? Do you want a robot to serve you dinner at a restaurant, take your temperature at a hospital, or decide based on an algorithm and social credit score that you've exceeded your energy allowance for the month and you find your heat turned off remotely—and with no human to talk to, to rectify the situation?

These are just a few examples of how Pluto could use his bulldozer of doom to challenge us to decide if we collectively (through laziness, fear, denial) hand over the keys to our humanity to cyberoverlords and become cyborgs, losing the most precious thing we have: *our freedom to be ourselves.*

To reference Emerson again:

> *Do you want to be a power in the world? Then be yourself. Be true to the highest within your soul and then allow yourself to be governed by no customs or conventionalities or arbitrary man-made rules that are not founded on principle.*

And believe it: some technological overseers want to govern every aspect of our lives. Pluto's transit through Aquarius may bring us face-to-face with the "dark side" of this technological control bearing down on us in more areas of daily life. What may start as a convenience can turn into a chokehold. Will you let it? Technology has its place, but in this author's opinion, it is no substitute for what it means to be human, "true to the highest within your soul."

Technology, of course, is not inherently evil. I am truly hopeful that whatever innovations arise when Pluto in Aquarius trines Uranus in Gemini will be ones that help humanity, rather than the opposite. These dates are:

July 18, 2026
November 29, 2026
June 15, 2027
January 13, 2028
May 10, 2028

Ultimately, Pluto's transit through Aquarius is likely to change our world through dismantling previous "old school" ways of doing things, bring in shiny (but coldly mechanical replacements), and then create a situation of ultimate reckoning when we will have to decide how far do we veer away from our birthright to live according to the highest human principles, rather than let our souls be lost forever in cyberspace, in a virtual reality that is devoid of true human connection.

March 1, 2036 may sound like a long time into the future—and it kinda is. That is when Pluto will move into the final decan (last ten degrees) of Aquarius, when the regeneration phase kicks into full gear. Who knows what the world will look like then. That part of the story is still unwritten, but astrology gives an indication of what potential exists—and reminds us that the stakes are significant.

***

In terms of using Pluto in Aquarius energies in your life, ponder upon this quote from writer D.H. Lawrence:

> *Sometimes snakes can't slough. They can't burst their old skin. Then they go sick and die inside the old skin, and nobody ever sees the new pattern. It needs a real desperate recklessness to burst your old skin at last. You simply don't care what happens to you, if you rip yourself in two, so long as you do get out.*

Pluto doesn't meet you halfway: It's all or nothing. But remember, his ultimate mission is to heal and regenerate—and he will put the pressure on you to do so, until you feel that "desperate recklessness" to set yourself free. Although innovative, Aquarius is a fixed sign, which means once they've found some approach that works, they usually stick with it. Pluto's transit through Aquarius is saying that your future requires a new approach. Irregardless of whatever unique way worked up to this point, going forward will require something new and radically different from you—Pluto will see to it.

Back on December 21, 2020, a new 20-year cycle began when Jupiter met up with Saturn at one degree of Aquarius. Jupiter is the planet of opportunity, and Saturn is the planet of manifestation. We need both to create and commit; we need possibilities to open up and discipline to do the work and make something of those fortunate lucky breaks—and to manifest our greatness. Whatever "house" one degree Aquarius occupies in your natal chart is a focus for personal growth for two decades.

As Pluto transits over this degree, he triggers that Jupiter/Saturn energy. Transits in 2021 and 2022 brought you face to face with some harsh realities and choices in the Aquarian area of your chart—all leading to this moment. You were preparing the ground for Pluto in Aquarius. Now that he's here, it's time to step into your future—leaving behind the old ways, the old identities, the old patterns. Pluto will be in Aquarius for the remainder of the 20-year Jupiter/Saturn cycle.

Pluto will exactly activate the Jupiter/Saturn conjunction in February 2024 when he finally reaches one degree Aquarius; however, his influence is so tectonic that we are likely to feel this "triggering" energy from the end of March 2023 to mid-June 2023.

And true to form, Pluto is likely to make you feel like that reckless snake at the above-referenced times, with immense pressure to release yourself from restrictions—whatever they may be. Radical actions may be necessary (although they perhaps appear "reckless" to outside observers who think you've gone "rogue"—you know the truth). You've got to save yourself and get out before the situation sucks the last drop of Life from your Soul.

As I stated in my intro, luck most often stems from Awareness, Alignment, Action, and Alchemy. The last few years have brought you enough discomfort to be aware of what needs changing in your life; now, Pluto insists you align and take action. His alchemy will transform your life from the ground up—and bring immense, powerful healing during the next 20 years, as follows:

ARIES: Pluto transits your eleventh house of hopes, wishes, dreams—Reinvent your life and use your talents in ways that are truly ground-breaking. Push through the discomfort of leaving those behind who do not understand this "mission critical" in your life. New and better alliances will be formed. You could become a major player/agent of change in the world, a relentless champion of the Truth. If the Empire Strikes Back, you'll be on the front lines doing what you can to mobilize the forces of good.

TAURUS: Pluto transits your tenth house of career and status—Face the nervousness you might feel about leaving behind a career or relationship you've outgrown. False narratives need to be called out—tell yourself the truth about what you really need. Pluto will make you face power dynamics in this area of life—not to make you miserable, I assure you—but rather to show you where you must rise to the occasion and show who's boss; if someone has consistently been taking advantage of you, that situation is likely to come to a head in true point-of-no-return Plutonic fashion. Let's hope it doesn't get to that point because a raging bull can do a lot of damage.

GEMINI: Pluto transits your ninth house of the big picture perspective—Accept that you need more from the world, yes, but also realize the world needs more from you (via sharing your talents and gifts). You become even more connected with your spirituality and the quest to "find yourself." Take action to journey forth on re-discovering who you are and what matters most. After Uranus enters your sign, Geminis will lead society into this brave, new technological age; consider carefully how you will do so and still keep your integrity.

CANCER: Pluto transits your eighth house of transformation—*What doesn't kill you makes you stronger*, but you're tired of singing that song of endurance. Release the "make do" mindset; Pluto's leading you on a journey of radical empowerment to be ruthless in pursuing that which brings your spirit happiness. Trust yourself and dive into the deep end of your soul. When it comes to transforming your life, Pluto will guide you through overcoming your resistance to following your more eccentric desires. Can you be less judgmental about embracing your "nerdy" side?

LEO: Pluto transits your seventh house of relationships (both business and personal)—You're no beast of burden, Leo—yet more often than not, certain people take advantage of your good nature and give you little in return. Not that you're keeping score, necessarily, but ... you need reciprocal acts of love and service in your life. Pluto will empower you to banish takers from your kingdom or queendom. Have the courage to distinguish beasts from beauties—and banish accordingly. And also look at your own "stuff" when it comes to wanting absolute control in your associations; it's not about having power *over*, but having power *with*. Better and more authentic relationships will eventually emerge during this transit.

VIRGO: Pluto transits your sixth house of work and well-being—Face the fact that you need to say "no" more often—and with the tone of voice that says you mean business. Then say "yes" more to your own priorities (and then actually put yourself at the top of your agenda). No more doing things for the sake of appearances. Accept the fact that your opinion is what matters most when you look in the mirror. Pluto will help you transform the Virgoan idea of "service"—the very word implies a hierarchy of master/servant—into one of *sharing*—a word that empowers you to decide who gets what from you—and who doesn't.

LIBRA: Pluto transits your fifth house of love, romance, creativity—and the saying *to love the bones of* someone comes to mind (and it sounds very Plutonian to me)—as if there were such a thing as a "psychic x-ray" that allowed you to see the shape and quality of a person's soul. During this transit, Pluto will require you to see beyond surfaces into the interior workings of your relationships—with others, but also with yourself. While the fifth house is associated with pleasure and play, Pluto's transit is likely to feel heavy in this house as he brings to your awareness how you may have been skating along on life's edges, not fully participating, perhaps because of a fear of failure or of being hurt. Pluto will bulldoze you into a corner so that you must reckon with the question: what will it take for you to overcome your fears so that you *live deep and suck out all the marrow of life* (Thoreau)?

SCORPIO: Pluto transits your fourth house of home, family, roots—No matter where you go, there you are. How is this so? Because your heart goes with you. And while you can have a change of heart—choosing different priorities and destinations over others—one thing is consistently true: love is what opens the door to your heart. And to be honest, yours is often only open a crack, Scorpio—because it takes a lot for you to trust that someone isn't going to come in and trash the place you call home. Take action on sweeping clean the threshold and oiling that old lock. Ready yourself for welcoming in strangers who will reveal themselves as soul family. Wherever you end up during this Pluto transit (and a significant move of residence could occur), home will be where a brand new story begins.

SAGITTARIUS: Pluto transits your third house of communication—the mind is a terrible thing to waste, and you have one of the most brilliant minds out there, Sagittarius. Don't waste your words on the air, but commit them to shareable form—podcast, blog, book, film, poem, song. Face any tendencies to fritter away your time in frivolous communications and mindless scrolling on social media. Take action on your "truth telling" project—and start first with yourself. Your words have power; use them wisely.

CAPRICORN: Pluto transits your second house of money and values—Yes, you love your pentacles, certificates of achievement, and gold trophies—that is not likely to ever change, nor should it. Your striving for the mountaintop inspires the rest of us to do better. Here's the thing, however: Pluto is going to wreck your best-laid plans IF (and notice how I capitalized that!) said plans are not aligned with the highest and best Capricornian values of loyalty, integrity, practicality, patience, and hard work. In other words, Pluto will wrecking ball any project conceived solely in self-interest and executed with speed that compromises quality. This saying comes to mind: *If you give a man a fish, th you feed him for a day. If you teach a man to fish, you feed him for a lifetime.* Teach others through your living example that prosperity and abundance come to those who create something of lasting value not only for themselves, but also for others.

AQUARIUS: Pluto transits your first house of the self—I suggest getting yourself a copy of Robert Greene's *The 48 Laws of Power* to guide you through this transit, which will heighten in intensity as Pluto reaches the degree of your Sun (which you would need to find on your birth chart and then consult an ephemeris to determine—or book a Soul Session with me on my website, and I can tell you!). Now, while I don't recommend seducing, charming, and deceiving people to gain the upper hand, all of which Greene's book discusses, I do believe this book will help you consider your own definition of power and what it means to use it righteously in the world. Pluto through your first house shines a spotlight on those nooks and crannies of life where you've perhaps given your power away to others, or simply neglected using it at all. Face the fact that you have an important purpose in life to be a champion for noble causes, but first you must ennoble yourself by claiming your crown of power—and wearing it proudly.

PISCES: Pluto transits your twelfth house of your inner world—Churning up the waters of your subconscious, Pluto renders you intimately familiar with the River Styx, the body of water that separates the living from the dead in Greek mythology. You could find yourself floating between these worlds, as Pluto stirs up memories of your own past lives, and reconnects you through the astral plane with ancestors, spirit guides, and ascended masters. As your subconscious is stirred, visions and dreams heal old issues and help you release karmic baggage (some of which you could have been carrying for lifetimes). Trust in what you are being shown in this private "Spirit School." And tap into Pluto's power to translate—as you see fit—these astral encounters into Art that brings people to the ineffable—an emotional reaction so profound that they have no words for it.

7

Mercury Retrograde in Earth Signs

MERCURY RETROGRADE OCCURS IN in earth signs this year, suggesting that you will be reviewing how certain areas in your life have been flourishing—or not. It's time to reassess methods for fertilizing, growing, and nurturing situations in whatever house the Mercury retrograde energy influences in your natal chart.

Mercury rules your communication style, the way your mind works, how you like to gather and process information, how you set intentions and make plans, and even how you "sell" your ideas and persuade people to your way of thinking. In general, Mercury impacts transportation, marketing, media, publishing, writing, contracts, teaching, and self-expression and the tangible things in life that support those endeavors (texts, emails, computers, cars, documents, websites, classes, cell phones, etc.) Mercury loves speed, so when it goes retrograde, Mercury likes to express his crankiness at the slowdown by causing mischief and mayhem with the aforementioned situations.

In earth signs, Mercury has a tendency to slow his roll a little bit (even when going direct). Mercury in Taurus, Virgo, or Capricorn promotes *thoroughness* and *practicality*. Whatever information is gathered is sorted and parsed with those qualities in mind. While earth energy can be patient, earth signs can sometimes be stubborn and inflexible, so Mercury retrograde in Taurus, Virgo, and Capricorn can help you review where you might need to bring more flexibility to your life and consider alternative viewpoints and solutions.

Because Mercury goes retrograde three times a year for three weeks at a time, you simply can't afford to wait around for his retrograde temper tantrum to pass. You can still be productive during a Mercury retrograde by using the energies to slow down and re-assess, revise, and reformulate a plan for wherever the transit is occurring in your chart. Here's the scoop on how to do that for each Mercury retrograde period for 2023:

Mercury Retrograde in Capricorn - December 29, 2022 to January 18, 2023

(Note: Mercury is also retrograde from December 13 to January 1, 2024 in Capricorn and Sagittarius, so the following information is applicable at that time as well.)

ARIES: What is or is not working in your career? Revisit and finish work projects. Reconnect with networks, former colleagues, etc. Review career goals and what steps toward success you can take in the year ahead. An offer from the past could resurface now. Before saying yes, evaluate its worth to your life in solid, practical terms. A pro/con list written down on paper may be helpful now. Let the quality of feeling in your body as you handwrite the list help you decide.

TAURUS: How might you need to re-envision your life and re-write your five-year plan? Rethink where you are going in your life and who's along for the ride. Revisit dreams for long-distance travel and come up with a plan to make it happen (but don't book tickets, etc. until after the retrograde is over).

GEMINI: How are you proceeding with your personal transformation and healing goals? What tweaks may need to be made? A good time to review budgets, savings, and investment plans and for researching solutions to long-standing issues. Mars retrograde in your sign until January 12 encourages you to look at what is working in your life and what is not, and the Mercury retrograde can help you rethink how you can get your needs met.

CANCER: Are your relationships all that you want them to be? What former relationship themes/issues/people are coming up for review? Reconnect with people who are good for you. Renegotiate business contracts and "terms" of personal associations. Resolve to be better with your boundaries going forward. Pluto has certainly taught you a lot about relationships since 2008, and this Mercury retrograde can help you put all those lessons into perspective.

LEO: What is unsettled about your work life? What needs to change? Reconsider your work/life balance and career goals. It's a good time to return to the gym, review your diet, and re-commit to personal health regimens. Use the retrograde period to complete work tasks that have been on the back burner.

VIRGO: What are you giving your life force energy to? Do you still feel aligned and connected to your personal projects? It may be appropriate now to resurrect a creative project from your "someday" files and breathe new life into it. Old flames could reconnect now, but make sure they've really changed before you get too involved.

LIBRA: What changes need to be made in the home? What family issues are still unresolved? It's time to see where cracks in the foundation exist (perhaps literally) and make a plan for fixing them once Mercury goes direct. Review your support systems to ensure that you have what you need to make progress on your goals.

SCORPIO: What conversation needs to happen between you and someone else due to unfinished business? How can you raise your awareness of your personal messaging so that you can be a more effective writer, speaker, teacher, salesperson, etc. This is a good time to rework a writing project, re-do your website, revamp your branding.

Reconnecting with siblings (whether blood family or those you've chosen to be your family) is also favored at this time.

SAGITTARIUS: How can you review your budget for leaks and cut unnecessary expenses? Reconsider monthly subscriptions, recurring charges, that type of thing. Set up systems for accounting, banking, automatic bill paying to make your life easier. Revisit if you are aligned energetically with the investment of time and energy your goals may require of you in 2023. Adjust accordingly.

CAPRICORN: Where do you need to revamp your personal appearance and style to match your new vibration and direction in life? It's time for Capricorn 2.0 - a new and improved version of yourself to present to the world. Clean out your closets and drawers to welcome in an upgraded wardrobe (purchased after Mercury goes direct). Review your goals and decide if they still excite you. Re-adjust accordingly and make a plan to work toward those things that bring you the most joy in 2023.

AQUARIUS: In what ways are you rethinking some deep issues in your life? Congratulate yourself for the profound psychological healing you've been doing since 2008 and re-affirm what's important to you. Release the last bits of emotional baggage or literal baggage in the form of clutter that no longer serves you. You don't need to wait until March to do a spring cleaning of your surroundings.

PISCES: How can you rethink your methods for manifesting some cherished dreams? What are the practical structures and systems you need to make your life run more smoothly? This is a good time to reconnect with old friends and/or a network or organization you've belonged to previously. Make a vision board for your year ahead and combine it with a monthly checklist of tasks to keep you on track for making your wishes come true in 2023.

Mercury Retrograde in Taurus - April 21 to May 14

ARIES: Are you spending your money wisely? Review your inflow and outflow, set up budgets, cut unnecessary expenses. If extra bounty comes in, do you have a plan to secure your wealth? If you have a plan, does that plan need a few tweaks? You will want to lay the groundwork for solid financial management in preparation for Jupiter entering your second house of money right after the Mercury retrograde is over. Do your research on financial advisors, investments, banks, accountants, etc.

TAURUS: Where do you need to revamp your personal appearance and style to match your new vibration and direction in life? As Uranus shakes up your sign, you may be drawn to a radically different presentation of self in everyday life. Reflect on what is and what is not working for you in terms of how you show up in the world. Release whatever represents an old identity, role etc. and after Mercury goes direct, buy yourself at least one item that celebrates the new you.

GEMINI: Uranus has been shaking and stirring up Taurus, your house of the subconscious, for a while now, bringing all sorts of awareness to your life. You've been putting things into perspective and releasing lots of emotional baggage, limiting beliefs, and old karma. With Mercury retrograde in Taurus, your twelfth house, take a moment to reflect upon your progress. An old psychological issue may come up for review now, for a final and ultimate release and healing. You've got this.

CANCER: It's time to put the finishing touches on a creative project, one that could bring you substantial gains. Aim for May 26 (after the Mercury retrograde) to make manifest a most precious dream when Venus in your sign will be in favorable alignment to Uranus in Taurus. This Mercury retrograde helps you make sure you have what you need in place to take advantage of the transits later in May. Upon reflection, you may make a surprising choice that helps you better connect with the energies of prosperity.

LEO: Remember that work stuff you were re-examining when Mercury was retrograde in Capricorn? Well, it comes up for review now again, but this time, you're solidifying a plan. Mars is getting ready to enter your sign on May 20, right after the retrograde, and this is a significant time of energetic reboot for you when you are fired up and ready to take on the world. Jupiter will be moving into your career zone as of May 16, a few days after the retrograde is over, bringing you expansive opportunities and helping you get unstuck from lingering career delays, disappointments, and dramas. Use the Mercury retrograde in your Taurus career zone to rethink and re-envision what you want from the career sector of your chart...and how you want to be recognized for your efforts.

VIRGO: Mercury retrograde in your ninth house of travel supports revisiting a place that is like a second home for you, an environment that brings out the lush, sensual side of your nature, a verdant zen oasis. Such a lovely time out can help you reconsider the bigger picture of your life and your overall satisfaction. This is also a good time to redesign your website (if you have one), edit a book you've been working on, and rebalance your chakras (spiritual tune-up). An unexpected invitation from a connection you haven't heard from in a while could also manifest at this time.

LIBRA: Uranus in Taurus over the last few years has brought intense, transformational situations to your world, often out of nowhere. Yes, crisis can bring opportunity, but it often takes time to come to terms with sudden and disruptive upheavals—especially when those involve other people's resources, intimacy, and endings you weren't quite ready for—before you can take advantage of any silver lining that might exist. Someone may resurface in your life during the Mercury retrograde to put the final "karmic wrap up" on one of these Uranian upheavals. Or perhaps you finally have a big rethink about what all went down and, as a result, you're able to put the situation behind you once and for all. If a significant other (whether in a business or romantic sense) reappears now, just know it is likely to be a fleeting visit; they could be checking in just for an ego boost to see if you still care. Do you?

SCORPIO: When the karma is done, the relationship is over, and someone from your past may be coming back around, reminding you why you ended it in the first place. And maybe you need that reminder in order to cut that last thread of connection that was keeping you from moving on. As I mention in the chapter in this book about Uranus, you have some excellent transits for calling in new relationships (whether business or personal), so let this Mercury retrograde in your seventh house of relationships help you put a former association firmly behind you, rather than up close and personal again in your life. If you need a reminder of why you let them go, write down all the reasons why in black and white. And then burn that paper (safely, of course).

SAGITTARIUS: You've been undergoing surprising changes with your work and well-being courtesy of Uranus in Taurus, your sixth house. During this Mercury retrograde, re-examine your work schedule and revamp your health routines. This energy is excellent for making a to-do list and getting things done that have been hanging over your head and causing you stress. You may reconnect with former work colleagues, clients, contacts. Doing so may open a door of opportunity for you after the retrograde is over and Jupiter transits Taurus after May 16.

CAPRICORN: This Mercury retrograde in your fifth house encourages you to revisit a creative project, as it has enormous potential. On May fifth, when Venus in Gemini (your sixth house of work) receives a supportive kiss from Jupiter in Aries, you may fall in love with this project all over again, and finish it with delight and pride (this is also the day of the full moon lunar eclipse in Scorpio, your eleventh house of hopes, wishes, and dreams). Revisiting and completing this project can bring enormous gains to your life and it/you could be the talk of the town. Old flames could reconnect now, but think twice before you consider re-engaging. You've got too much good juju to channel into a significant achievement now to fritter your time away with a fly-by-night, hit-it-and-quit-it distraction—unless you want to be distracted, which is altogether your choice.

AQUARIUS: Since May 15, 2018, Uranus has been moving through your fourth house of home, family, and foundation. This transit often suddenly uproots us from places we've lived for years (perhaps since 2000 when Jupiter and Saturn had their "great conjunction" in Taurus). You may move a few times during a Uranian transit of your fourth house before settling on the right place for you to build anew. The Mercury retrograde in Taurus could have you rethinking where you're living, how you're living, and who you're living with...and if recent changes have been to your liking. You may need to renegotiate terms of a lease now, or terms of a living arrangement, or you may need to repair something in your home that wasn't fixed correctly the first time around.

PISCES: Uranus in Taurus since 2018 has been delivering you downloads of genius ideas, some of which you've been able to make use of, and others not (because there's only so many hours in a day). At times you're even surprised by the wild and witty bon mots that spring from your lips and electrify your audience. During this Mercury retrograde in Taurus, you could be reconfiguring a writing, teaching, speaking, or sales project to showcase more of your originality. Uranus has been helping you reconnect with the power of your innovative mind, and the Mercury retrograde can help you put the dazzling touches on an important effort. Someone from your past may serve as a significant sounding board and give helpful advice.

Mercury Retrograde in Virgo - August 23 to September 15

Note: Both Mercury in Virgo and Venus in Leo will be retrograde from August 23 to September 4. Retrograde periods can bring frustration and delays, and with this double whammy retrograde energy, please be especially mindful of the details when it comes to love and money transactions. The terms of the relationship or the terms of the contract may be unclear or could get changed after the retrogrades are over. Information can sometimes be withheld or hard to obtain or decipher, and hidden agendas abound.

ARIES: It's time for a check-up of your heart—maybe a literal visit to the cardiologist to make sure everything is tickety-boo, and/or a literal check-in with yourself and how you're feeling about the quality and quantity of joyful connections and pleasurable activities in your life. Are there too many emotional vampires in your life? One may come back from the dead to haunt you now. Mars (your ruling planet) will enter Libra on August 27, so re-examine where stress in romantic relationships takes a toll on you, and try not to let someone goad you into an argument and manipulate you with a guilt trip. You could really benefit from a time-out in some little cabin in the woods now, and let the greenery bring a soothing calm to your heart chakra.

TAURUS: A battle of wills when it comes to making changes on the home front is likely during this retrograde—whether you're arguing with someone for the umpteenth time about leaving the toilet seat up, or having a spirited discussion about their aesthetically unappealing collection of _____ (fill in the blank) which they insist on displaying proudly on your antique coffee table—a renegotiation may be necessary. An old paramour may pluck at your heartstrings now, but proceed with caution (if you proceed at all). Maybe just enjoy the flattery. You're in major re-evaluation mode when it comes to what is worth giving your time and attention to. The full moon in Pisces on August 31 may provide illumination on whether you should continue to give your heart to a relationship or situation, but wait until after September 15 to move ahead on whatever you decide.

GEMINI: A home or family matter may need your attention, but it could be challenging to come to a solution that suits your finances or the fancy of those involved. Trying to get hold of someone to come out to the house to fix whatever needs fixing may also be fraught with miscommunications, misunderstandings, missed phone calls, etc. Get everything in writing and double-check service contracts. If you need to purchase a big ticket item for the home, try to wait until after September 15...or even a few days after that. The new moon in Virgo (your fourth house) will happen on September 15, and it's auspicious to begin a new home-related project using that energy. Try to be patient and understanding in conversations with those close to you as you renegotiate terms of the relationship—or who does what around the house.

CANCER: You may be going over old ground when it comes to finances, and there may be a conversation you've had before with a significant other about family finances that resurfaces for another go-round. In general, it's better to avoid big-ticket item purchases when both Venus and Mercury are retrograde, so please keep that advice in mind. An excellent use of this energy would be to re-negotiate terms of a financial obligation; think debt consolidation, refinancing, etc. Do the necessary research and call the appropriate people to gather the information you need, and then make it happen after September 15. You may also want to formulate a plan for getting more money out of your employer or from your own business; aim for the full moon in Aries (your career house) on September 29 for achieving results here.

LEO: The emphasis is front and center on your finances and goals; however, it's a time for review, not for splashing the cash. With Venus retrograde in your sign, everything in your life is up for re-evaluation, especially your career (Venus rules your tenth house). Mercury retrograde in your house of money and values suggests that as you re-calibrate your life priorities, your financial priorities will shift, too. What are you willing to do, career-wise, to manifest more money? Raise your value in your own eyes and ask for more...after the retrogrades have passed. And with Mercury retrograde in the cash zone, you want to be very mindful of any bank mix-ups, over-charges, etc. Monitor your accounts closely.

VIRGO: You could benefit from some serious self-care during this Mercury retrograde in your own sign, and I don't mean just a spa day, although that is certainly something you need and deserve. It's an optimal time to pause and regroup and recharge in order to rethink your longer term goals. You need some fresh air, clear-headed solitude, your journal, and a nice cup of tea to jot down ideas of what you'd like to focus on over the next nine months—not just in terms of worldly achievement, but also in terms of nurturing your own soul. The new moon in your sign occurs on September 15 right after the Mercury retrograde is over. Take action and plant a beautiful dream seed then.

LIBRA: You're in need of a mental break although your DMs may be blowing up with messages from former friends, lovers, colleagues, associates you thought you would never hear from again. Subconscious patterns of thinking/communicating may get triggered by a certain person's name appearing in your socials or texts. What you thought was finished (relationships, yes, but also personal projects) likely is not. Whatever or whomever resurfaces now offers you an opportunity to gain mental clarity and perspective on the past—and what you may still need to heal and release. The significance of this transit is not so much about reconnecting with someone from long ago, but instead reconnecting with *yourself* and what that person has taught you about your communication style and the ability to get your needs met in a healthy (non co-dependent) way.

SCORPIO: As you look for ways to improve your financial remuneration from your career activities, never under-estimate the power of good old-fashioned face-to-face networking. This is a good time to reconnect with professional groups and associations you've been a part of before and attend one of their events. (Travel during Mercury retrograde usually goes okay when we revisit a place we've been previously.) A helpful mentor from your past may give you solid advice now and/or an introduction that could help you in your career. Re-evaluate your financial compensation and decide on a plan to help you bring more money into your world. September 16 (after the retrograde is over) is a favorable time to have an important meeting to discuss such matters (such as asking for a raise).

SAGITTARIUS: Roll up your shirtsleeves, Sadge, because you're getting stuck in to some impressive work initiative this month. You're likely pushing hard to put the finishing touches on a manuscript, course, advertising campaign, website, or invention. Whatever you're doing, you identify strongly with it—so strongly, in fact, that it may be a good idea to take a step back during the retrograde and rethink what your audience/client/customer needs from your brainchild. When we're so immersed in a project, it can be challenging to see informational gaps that may need to be filled in or tweaks that could be made to make the user experience easier. You'll do that now. After the new moon in your Virgo career zone on September 15 would be a beneficial time to launch your creation to the world.

CAPRICORN: Your goals are never far from your mind, are they Capricorn? And this Mercury retrograde is no different. You're in major rethink mode about the bigger picture perspective of your life and you're doing a lot of soul searching now, re-evaluating the changes you've made thus far this year and if they've been "worth it." A weekend away to a place you've been before can help you clear your mind and re-focus. You may be mulling over a commitment (whether business or personal) and if you want to pull the plug and move on. Jupiter going retrograde on September 4 in your fifth house of love, romance, and creative life force energy encourages your rethink along practical lines. If the person or situation in question is not adding to your life in positive ways, then what's the point?

AQUARIUS: Where attention goes, energy flows, and your attention during this retrograde is on the resources you share with others. Your desk may be piled high with paperwork and research materials to help you secure funding, manage an inheritance/estate, re-mortgage your house, repay your debts, etc. You may be revisiting an intimate personal matter in a close relationship, perhaps even reconnecting with an ex—there may be one last karmic puzzle piece to put into place with this person before you decide what's done is done. You may feel you simply do not have the energy nor will to continue to try to come to an understanding with this person. As long as you're clear in your own mind, that's all that matters—and you can let go with love.

PISCES: The emotional stakes are high during this retrograde, as someone(s) from your past (either love or business—or both!) could circle back and leave you in a quandary as to their sincerity. You want to believe them, but...right in the middle of the retrograde, on August 31, is your full moon, and it's conjunct retrograde Saturn. The moon conjunct Saturn can bring a situation that weighs heavy on your heart, because it is likely Déjà vu all over again as history repeats itself. Don't beat yourself up for someone else's shenanigans—or be disappointed if they are simply not capable of (or responsible enough) to give you what you want (and deserve). Do not be tempted to lower your standards.

Reminder: Mercury is also retrograde from December 13 to January 1, 2024 in Capricorn and Sagittarius. See the previous entry on Mercury retrograde in Capricorn from the beginning of 2023 for insight.

8

Jupiter Transits Taurus: Golden Opportunities

JUPITER ENTERS TAURUS ON May 16, 2023, and will be going direct at full power until September 4 through December 30, when he'll be retrograde. As previously noted, Jupiter is about expansion and limitless possibilities, and in Taurus, he wants to deliver the tangible, golden goods. Ruled by Venus, Taurus appreciates the finer things in life and as the domicile of the second house in the general astrological wheel, Taurus is about your money, resources, values, security and safety needs, and self-esteem.

Jupiter in Taurus reminds you that what you desire also desires you. Joy is an aphrodisiac that amplifies the law of attraction. Money is, after all, simply energy, and Jupiter in Taurus encourages you to do what you love to create the prosperity you seek. You don't want to be a person who "knows the price of everything and the value of nothing" (the definition of a 'cynic' as penned by author and playwright Oscar Wilde). Indeed, cynicism is the antithesis of Jupiterian energy. Jupiter in Taurus reminds us of the value of investing our time and energy into happy pursuits, to be patient and kind with ourselves as we grow into our greatness. When you truly love yourself (Venus) and proceed in your endeavors with a loving heart, you shift your energetic frequency. In so doing, you create a more optimal environment for abundance to manifest.

The key with this transit is not to simply pursue wealth for wealth's sake, but rather to pursue the energy of wealth creation—which is love. Jupiter can bring faith to your life—and help you believe that you are worthy of life's golden opportunities. And this transit should give you plenty of those if you understand and work with the spiritual vibration of wealth creation. The feel good factor comes first, and then the money will follow.

Here's how these golden opportunities may manifest for you when Jupiter is in Taurus from May 16, 2023 to May 25, 2024:

ARIES: Golden opportunities may manifest for you in terms of manifesting more money, getting paid what you are worth, taking on a project that you believe in—and that rewards you in cold, hard cash and kudos from the public. Live by your values, and you enhance your good fortune. Earmark some funds for a travel adventure you can take when Mars transits Sagittarius from November 24 to January 4, 2024. You are worthy to receive all good things, so welcome them into your life with open arms and a grateful heart.

TAURUS: Golden opportunities may manifest for you when it comes to being in the right place at the right time. You're on everyone's guest list, the phone is ringing off the hook, and you feel like you can take on the world—and there could be a significant trip that brings a new important connection to your life or strengthens an ongoing relationship. The power of your kindness and patience is rewarded now in the form of karmic payback, and you could be on the receiving end of grand gestures and pledges of loyalty. Someone really shows up for you, in other words. You deserve this fresh start!

GEMINI: Golden opportunities may manifest for you in terms of behind-the-scenes support, someone putting in a good word for you without your knowledge, a karmic reward for past times when you were the one giving the assistance to a person who needed it. You may feel as though you have an angel on your shoulder steering you toward opportunity's doorstep, as the most amazing synchronicities and lucky breaks could happen when you trust your urges to go off the beaten path, as it were. You benefit from time spent in quiet contemplation, tuning into the gifts of your soul—of which there are many.

CANCER: Golden opportunities may manifest for you when it comes to sharing your talents with the wider world (and yes, that includes getting paid for said talents!). You gain from teaching, learning, writing, speaking, nurturing your creativity—and making connections that support you in those endeavors. A wise and influential friend could be made during this transit. Normally quite shy, you feel a kindred soul vibe with this person, and so come out of your shell more easily than usual. Together, the two of you are a living example of the power of friendship.

LEO: Golden opportunities may manifest for you in your career and status—and they are well-deserved. During Jupiter's transit in Taurus, you could get a plum position that raises your professional profile and that fills your bank account with more money than you've seen in a while. While Uranus's transit through your career zone has brought sudden changes the last several years, now beneficial Jupiter could show you why certain career situations shifted the way they did (in order to pave the way for this Jupiter transit). Career-wise, Jupiter could replace in grand fashion whatever might have been "lost" by Uranus. Also, "status" includes marriage, and you could meet a potential life-mate now, or perhaps renew your vows on a second honeymoon. You are a shining star!

VIRGO: Golden opportunities may manifest for you to travel abroad, to earn a college degree, to start or manage a web-based business, to write a best-selling book, and to finish certain important goals to great satisfaction. Jupiter in Taurus encourages you to believe in yourself more than you ever have before. You can transcend any limiting beliefs or circumstances that kept you playing small on the stage of life. You are replenished spiritually via diverse cultural and intellectual experiences that lead you in new and beneficial directions. Adventure is your middle name.

LIBRA: Golden opportunities may manifest for you via other people and their "deep pockets." You could meet an important benefactor, get a mortgage, secure funding for a project, inherit, or possibly receive some other type of windfall. You may benefit from spiritual study—by diving deep into your soul and expressing your discoveries through writing, art, music, etc. You're unlocking hidden potential from your past lives, and in so doing, you bring healing to your life. You are a conduit for magic.

SCORPIO: Golden opportunities may manifest for you in relationships—whether business or personal. A significant connection—one who is generous, wise, funny, well-learned, and influential—can enter your life now. You may meet this person through travel or educational experiences and the excitement upon first meet will be palpable. A tower moment? Possibly, but in the best of ways: a *coup de foudre*, a love at first sight encounter. Indeed, if romance comes into your life, it could become an all-encompassing experience. Yes, even the most gothically-inclined Scorpios may suddenly abandon their penchant for moody solitude and solitary midnight walks along the moors, contemplating life's mysteries. But don't worry, darling—I still see you dressed all in black, svelte and sexy—with a huge smile on your face.

SAGITTARIUS: Golden opportunities may manifest for you to bring betterment to your life via home, garden, family, health, and healing. Any interest in starting a medicinal herb garden? You're feathering your nest, perhaps in anticipation of some new family commitment (marriage, baby, grand baby, pet, parent moving in). If you've been wanting a more steady work routine/schedule or a more reliable source of income, then Jupiter can help with that. You're continuing the "love trend" that Jupiter in Aries brought to your life; the Jupiter in Taurus energy helps you take practical steps to hold onto this happiness through better work/life balance, supportive home environment, and taking care of your health. You are Happiness personified!

CAPRICORN: Golden opportunities may manifest for you when it comes to pleasing yourself and following your Muse—and serious money could flow in as you share your creative genius with the public. Yes, the world is your oyster…and you could experience a regeneration of your love life as you rise like Venus from the half-shell in Botticelli's famous painting. Quite a few people could be awakening to your charms, Capricorn! You're not just flirting with fame and fortune during this transit, but also with real, live people! Your combination of dry humor, a wry smile, soulful eyes, a loyal heart, and high standards will magnetize the masses (or at least a few cutie pies). You are everyone's favorite now. Take time to savor the best that life has to offer you during this transit.

AQUARIUS: Golden opportunities may manifest for you to figure out where you truly belong—and with whom. You could travel to another state or country in order to investigate buying property; however, I encourage you to consider the vibe of the surroundings, not just whether or not it would make a good financial investment. As Pluto begins his transit of your sign, you will start to feel the unmistakable urge to transform your life from the ground up. You need to find the place where you see yourself growing your future. And while that type or foresight could be challenging for other signs, it's not for you—you have the uncanny ability to ascertain what's vibrating on the outer rings of psychic radar before it reaches the midpoint on the screen. Take Jupiter up on his opportunities to explore uncharted territory—whether that's a part of your current town you've never seen, or a city cross country that you've dreamed about for decades although you've never been. With this transit, you are in the perfect position to manifest your personal paradise.

PISCES: Golden opportunities may manifest for you in terms of improving your daily life with a new vehicle, connecting with like-minded friends for fun activities, and making a positive difference in your community through charitable activities. A sibling or soul brother/sister could be a source of stellar support for you in the year ahead. You are taking seriously your gifts in the communicative arts and could manifest an opportunity to display your work in a gallery, perform at a prestigious venue, and/or publish your writing to great acclaim. You are radiant with joy!

Note to all signs: When Jupiter is retrograde from September 4 through December 30, 2023, positive re-adjustments of your plans and projects may occur. This is the phase of keeping the faith and working toward your goals. Once Jupiter goes direct again, your efforts will bear their luscious, golden fruit.

9

Nodal Shift: A New Door Opens to a New Destiny

I LIKE TO DESCRIBE the North Node as a door that is destined to open at just the perfect time. (In fact, the north and south nodes are invisible points where the moon's orbit intersects the Earth's orbit around the sun.) On July 17, the North Node enters Aries, where it will stay until January 11, 2025. What is revealed beyond that door is a call to adventure, of boldly and bodaciously becoming a leader, a champion, a rebel with a very clear cause. The North Node in Aries encourages you to bust out and bust loose from pleasing others and instead focus on pleasing yourself for once. Be the hero or heroine of your life. Do for yourself what you so eagerly and wonderfully always do for others. Do it for you, and do it your way.

With the North Node in Aries, Fortune does indeed favor the bold. This transit rewards honesty, authenticity, independence, invention, calculated risk-taking, high energy, and self-expression. Don't be afraid to be different and/or be the first to pioneer a new way forward. You bring good luck to yourself during this transit when you are in the flow zone, immersed so intently in doing your thing that you lose all track of time. There is a certain rugged individualist vibe going on with this transit, so embrace it. Be very protective of your alone time so that you have the energy and space to birth something new in your world.

You may want to look back at the following time periods when Uranus was in Aries and what was suddenly, surprisingly and even shockingly transformed in your world at that time. The North Node transit of Aries can reveal a golden thread of karmic connection back to May 29, 2010 to August 14, 2010; March 13, 2011 to May 15, 2018; November 7, 2018 to March 6, 2019.

For example, in 2014 when Uranus went though my third house, I suddenly quit a job I had for 13 years and which involved a two-hour commute round trip every day. From then on, I've worked from home (third house is not only transportation/commute but how you live your daily life—Uranus changed up both for me in dramatic fashion). Now, the North Node transit through Aries may bring in a new opportunity for me that I could not have perhaps prepared for if I had still been stuck at that old job. That is what I mean by look back at the threads of experience...you can find clues as to how the energy might play out for you during this North Node transit.

The nodes work in pairs; we can't just mention the North Node without also checking in with the South Node, which will be in Libra. The South Node is a karmic release point, a "remembrance of things past," a story that's already been told. South Node transits can be especially "interesting" when they transit conjunct a personal planet.

So check and see if you have the Sun, Moon, Mercury, Venus, Mars in Libra. When the South Node conjuncts your Sun, you're likely leaving behind an identity you've outgrown. When the South Node conjuncts your Moon, you may leave behind a home, wrap up an intense relationship, make a significant emotional break with your past. When the South Node conjuncts your Mercury, you may be releasing old ideas, ways of communicating, thinking, etc. When the South Node conjuncts your Venus, there can be the ending of a karmic relationship, a monetary situation may come to a close (like changing jobs or finally paying off a debt). When the South Node conjuncts your Mars, you may release a habitual way of doing things, let go of some issue that has brought stress to your life, leave behind anger and frustration.

Here's how you might use the energies of the North Node transit in Aries and the South Node transit in Libra from July 17, 2023 until January 11, 2025:

ARIES: It's time to take a chance on yourself and show the world what you're made of. Don't hold back. Do the thing you were born to do, but try doing it a little differently. This is a time of major self-reinvention. You're loving the new you! At some point during this transit, you will fulfill a karmic contract of a business or personal nature. If you can, try to let go with love rather than burning bridges in glorious firebrand Aries fashion. You may go it alone for a while, but the Universe abhors a vacuum, and someone whose vibe is more aligned with yours is likely to manifest by the end of this transit—if that's what you want.

TAURUS: It's time to clear the cobwebs from your mind and shake the sleep out of your eyes. Listen to those whispers in the early dawn that are calling you to pastures new. A dream you thought would never see the light of day could be revived with gusto. Go for it! You are letting go of any person, place, situation that drains your energy and makes you doubt yourself. You bring healing benefit to yourself by changing up your daily schedule so that you have more "me" time; these changes may include freeing yourself from a dead-end job with toxic co-workers and negative vibes. You deserve better.

GEMINI: It's time to see where your visions and dreams can lead you. New faces, new places, new spaces: you're moving in different circles and changing up the cycles of your life. It's not change for change's sake, but because you truly need this. You are wrapping up one way of using your energy in the world in order to create something new—whether a book, a baby, or a business. Don't skip over the "tying up of loose ends" part—do make sure you mark this important rite of passage with some sort of ceremony.

CANCER: It's time to step into the limelight, the spotlight, the moonlight. You're on board with becoming the CEO of your Life. And you're doing it—whether in the boardroom or the bedroom—or from a little bungalow in Bali after you've retired. You have the power to reshape your destiny. As you finish a long cycle involving karmic family obligations, you will have more freedom and flexibility in your schedule to pursue a great adventure that is most likely connected with career. You may finally sell a house that was a money pit; the last "bird" flies the nest, leaving you more time for yourself; maybe you go back to work after a long time being at home (by choice or otherwise). Exciting!

LEO: It's time to make your presence known in the world, to publish a book, to travel abroad, to study something new, to expand your spiritual awareness. Let your light shine! Be brave in your pursuit of fresh horizons, even if getting out of the proverbial comfort zone scares you a little. You need the kind of excitement that this type of expansion brings to your heart, releasing you from a rut where you may have been overly attached to certain outcomes, people, situations, etc. — that you will see were not destined to materialize anyway. You're releasing a certain way you've seen the world, ending any type of anxious self-talk, and instead you are confidently expressing yourself without self-censorship (for fear "they" won't like what you have to say). Revolutionize the way you communicate with yourself first, and then watch the doors to destiny open for you as if by magic.

VIRGO: It's time to commit yourself to the deepest levels of healing, and the way you are likely to do so is by going on a shamanic quest to recall pieces of your Soul that have gotten displaced by trauma, loss, betrayal, mis-alignment, misunderstandings, etc., and re-integrate them into your life. In calling "lost" parts of yourself back to Center, you amplify your Power to direct your own life, to manifest that which is important to you. You are releasing the hold other people's energy may have had on you in terms of standards and expectations for living your life a certain way. Once you retrieve those missing pieces of your Soul's mosaic, you will align with greater creativity, prosperity, and purpose. You are realizing that yours is the only opinion that really matters when it comes to living a life that you love.

LIBRA: It's time to return to the Karmic School of Life and take a test. Resist the urge to look to others for the correct answers; you need to keep your eyes on your own paper. Since they have to do with your identity, these are questions only you can answer. If there are upheavals in relationships, they are more than likely a reflection of your own inner discontent. Once you deal with yourself, then you will find worldly success in the eyes of others, perhaps even those of a certain special someone. The North Node in your sign can bring new people into your life, but unless you work on changing yourself and letting go of old baggage when it comes to relating, these "new" relationships will just be more of the same old, same old—whether in a business or romantic sense.

SCORPIO: It's time to dive into the secrets of your subconscious in order to heal any tendencies to sacrifice your own best interests in the name of love, friendship, or "duty." You are releasing a tendency to beat yourself up over trying to reach self-imposed, impossibly high standards. Instead, you are embracing opportunities to connect with daily activities that bring you a sense of harmony and purpose; in fact, you may change jobs during this transit in order to find more personal fulfillment. Time spent in seclusion is best used in creative activities rather than in endless conversations with yourself that keep you stuck in an infinity loop of fear, doubt, and distraction.

SAGITTARIUS: It's time to embark upon one of the most prolific periods of your life—whether it's the fruit of your loins or the fruit of your imagination—you are birthing the new! One of the most important partnerships of your life may manifest during this transit. Whether you are creating a baby together or co-authoring a book together, you will have something tangible that manifests as a result of this connection. You may be tempted to speculate in your business, and while your instincts may be correct to do so, you will want to consider those speculations to involve working within a new network of associates. The well could have run dry, in other words, with your usual clients/contacts. You may benefit from ending certain professional associations that you may have outgrown. It's important not to count your pentacles before they've shown up in your paycheck; be prudent with your finances—even if you have a 'lucky streak' at some point during this North Node transit.

CAPRICORN: It's time to rebuild your life upon a strong foundation (now that Pluto is almost done with you) and now that the North Node is transiting your fourth house of home, family, and roots. At some point during this transit, you could improve your property, move to a place that is much more aligned for you (the mountains?), and/or create a happy home life. If your life situation warrants it, you could start a business from home or perhaps transition into working from home full-time. You may need to deal with changes in career; those changes are the Universe's way of bringing you back "home" to yourself. Your definition of success is likely to undergo a significant transformation; the south node releases you from public obligations that did not give you enough agency over your own life. You rebuild upon your own strength and power. The taste of personal victories is sweet: you find happiness at your own front door.

AQUARIUS: It's time to make a plan for what you can do daily to improve the future direction of your life. It's not a time of looking far and wide for answers, but rather looking within and communicating with those closest to you for inspiration and solutions. You have an opportunity to immerse yourself in all forms of media and communication in order to change the world for the better. You are a warrior for truth and justice through the power of your words. To be most effective, however, think in terms of the micro rather than the macro. For example, write a blog rather than novel; share your knowledge by speaking with a local community group rather than traipsing around the world racking up frequent flier miles in order to go to a conference. The same thing applies to improving your business if you have one: "word of mouth" marketing will be more successful for you than investing in a social media ad campaign.

PISCES: It's time to affirm the idea: *God Bless the Child that's got His Own.* The North Node opens multiple doors for you to meet influential people, to build your wealth, and to manifest your material desires. But you must bravely go forth and get your own blessings; it is through your courageous efforts that what you want can be yours. Beware the tendency to blame others for what you do not have; the responsibility rests firmly on your shoulders. The South Node transit through your eighth house helps you clear a karmic debt of long-standing. Do the right thing involving all tax, insurance, inheritance, mortgage, and legal matters. An intimate partnership that has hindered you from pursuing your own interests and/or that has been sexually unsatisfactory may dissolve during this transit. Do not be afraid to rebuild your life from a position of dedicated self-interest.

10

Venus Retrograde in Leo: Questions Only the Heart Can Answer

IN THE ZODIAC WHEEL, Leo rules the fifth house of love, romance, pleasure, hobbies, risk-taking, and creative life force energy. Leo represents the heart, gold, pride, generosity, and grand gestures. Venus in Leo loves to shine, to bask in the glow of compliments, to light up a room with her kindness, artistry, and innate ability to bring warm-hearted fun to interactions.

But when Venus goes retrograde in Leo from July 23 to September 4, the fire may temporarily gutter and reach a low point as you face questions only your heart can answer. Just as communications unravel or are delayed/misconstrued when Mercury goes retrograde, your feelings can unravel or face a reversal during a Venus retrograde. All that glitters is not gold, and you may face disappointing realities in love or in a venture whose rewards were paltry compared to the effort or risk involved. This is not a time to start a love affair, get engaged, get married or buy big ticket items. Additionally, don't break the bank on funding a new business and don't speculate to accumulate because your judgment and timing may be misguided.

The month of August is tricky with two full moons pushing your emotional buttons during the Venus retrograde. The first one is the full moon in Aquarius on August 1 squaring Jupiter in Taurus (ruled by Venus). Is someone trying to manipulate a situation using emotional/financial blackmail? Do relationships have too much of a *quid pro quo* / transactional feel about them for your liking? This "giving to get" attitude may be causing the discomfort. The full moon in Pisces on August 31 conjuncts Saturn in Pisces, and the emotional stakes are high: someone could be pushing for a love or financial commitment that you're hesitant to make (or you could be doing that to someone). Trust your intuition here, and revisit the situation once the retrograde is over. The timing may simply not be right for this major commitment now. *(Also see August's Monthly "Lucky Stars" for further insight on these energies.)*

The Venus retrograde in Leo suggests that you ask yourself if what you value, values you. Do people or situations steal your light or stoke your creative fires? What does your heart truly want? How can you bring more magic into your life through expressing your artistry? Reconsider your investments of time, money, and energy and if they still make you feel good, but decide who or what stays/goes after the retrograde is over.

Here's what to keep in mind during this Venus Retrograde in Leo:

ARIES: Venus retrogrades in your fifth house of love, romance, creativity, pleasure, and risk-taking. Your heart questions if a certain connection or project can sustain you in the long haul; are you (or the other person, if a romance) invested enough to see this situation through to its full development? With the North Node now in your sign, it could simply be that you are feeling the tug of destiny elsewhere. The grass isn't always greener, but in this case, it may be. Only you can decide, but take the time to sort through your feelings rather than making an impulsive decision that you will later regret.

TAURUS: Venus retrogrades in your fourth house of home, family, roots. Your heart may be questioning past events from childhood in order to put them into some sort of perspective, maybe in anticipation of a family reunion or travel to a place familiar to you from youth. You may be trying to assess if where and how you are currently living meets your needs. You may be going over old ground when it comes to family finances, budgets, mortgages, taxes, etc.—perhaps to determine if you should "love it or list it."

GEMINI: Venus retrogrades in your third house of communications and daily life. Your heart questions whether or not your words are adequate. You are the wordsmith *par excellence* of the zodiac, yet Venus retrograde could have your usual verbal facility fall flat. Someone could be signaling "talk to the hand" and be unmoved by your sentiments. Conversations about money and what you need from your relationship may go round in circles now—or, as previously stated—meet outright resistance. Your energy may be better spent on revaluing your priorities to decide which battles are worth fighting—and which ones you're unlikely to ever win. Keep an eye on your wallet during this transit—don't let stress mess with your head (as we tend to lose things when it does).

CANCER: Venus retrogrades in your second house of money and values. You're usually tuned in quite well to your enchanted grotto heart space, living with the mermaids as you do. But there may be an unsettled feeling during this transit, as if you've forgotten something important, a kind of temporary amnesia. You're combing the beach in search of treasure, when really you just need a quiet place to gaze at the full moon and face your inner tides, which have been tugging at you for a while now. Yes, you deserve all the riches in the world, but you want what you do for money to *matter*. Rethink how you can bring forth your inner pearls of wisdom, experience, and talent to those who will truly value them.

LEO: Venus retrogrades in your first house of the Self, including your physical body. Please, for the love of botox, do not make any major changes to your appearance during this transit: no new hairstyle, clothes, cosmetics, plastic surgery, etc. When Venus retrogrades in your first house, you can feel like you're the ugly duckling in a sea of supermodel beauties—I assure you, this is just Venus retrograde playing with your head—and then you go and do something drastic which you later regret and end up with a face looking like a boiled egg from too many fillers and laser treatments. Stop! A better use of this energy would be to affirm all you're grateful for in your world and take the focus off any (perceived) flaws that get magnified at this time.

VIRGO: Venus retrogrades in your twelfth house of "behind the scenes." A good use of this energy would be to hide yourself away in your studio to revisit a creative project and put the finishing touches on it, rather than entertaining ex-lovers in secret. But that's just my opinion. Your heart may have many questions about a previous relationship, and the karmic lessons you gleaned from it. This ex may not literally show up at your front door—but instead their presence could be poignantly felt in dreams, old letters you find stashed in a shoebox in your closet, a memory that pops up on your Facebook feed. Gain the closure you need during this transit, Virgo.

LIBRA: Venus retrogrades in your eleventh house of hopes, wishes, and dreams—and personal gains. Your heart has many questions about why some situations have worked out for you and others haven't. Venus is, after all, your ruling planet, so this transit is very personal. To get answers, you're likely to initiate contact with old flames, former bosses, long lost friends, childhood neighbors, and the like. But here's the thing: not everybody is going to be happy to hear from you. I'm not trying to be mean, honestly. Just know that your imperative to go over old ground and get whatever it is you're trying to get from doing so is *your* agenda—and no one needs to accommodate you. In fact, it may be better that they didn't. Look inside yourself first to determine why you have such a need to know the reasons why Fate moved in mysterious ways and then think twice before you make that call or send that text to those from the past whom you think owe you something. Pay more attention to the people in your life *now*.

SCORPIO: Venus retrogrades in your tenth house of career and status. You're wondering what you may need to tweak in order to manifest greater success—especially financially. Your heart is questioning whether you have the right to feel that work should be a pleasure, rather than a burden. You may have already achieved a certain level of success, and are wondering: well, how did I get here?—and, more importantly: do I want to stay? Remember, no rash moves during this transit. Use the time to revamp your CV, so if you decide to try make a change, you're ready to do so after Venus goes direct again.

SAGITTARIUS: Venus retrogrades in your ninth house of the big picture perspective of your life. Your heart wants to know if a certain relationship will be your "ride or die"—because you're having a hard time envisioning anything different, but you may not know where you stand. You have dreams of going the distance with this person, but you want to be sure. Or maybe you're not sure of your own feelings, as the North Node transiting through your Aries fifth house of romance may bring other options to your door. You may also be reworking a writing, internet, or teaching project; try to rethink its value proposition for your audience.

CAPRICORN: Venus retrogrades in your eighth house of transformation, shared resources, and psychic realms. All sorts of questions from the archive of your heart concerning the Plutonian underworld you've experienced since 2008 are in the frame; after all, this Venus retrograde is happening for you in Pluto's house. Eh, it's not your first rodeo revisiting issues of how other people treat you in intimate partnerships—whether we're talking the boardroom or the bedroom. But here's the thing: you're coming to the end of Pluto in your sign. You've done the work. When a connection from your past resurfaces to test your resolve, won't they be surprised to find the power dynamic has shifted. This Venus Retrograde puts you in the driver's seat of calling the shots with any ghosts from your past who think they can still haunt you.

AQUARIUS: Venus retrogrades in your seventh house of relationships, both business and personal. Your heart could be questioning why relationships often require so much negotiation. You keep telling them what you want and need—or do you? Are you even clear on what it is that you require from a certain relationship (whether business or personal) and *do you actually communicate that to the other person?* Half-truths, half sentences, half-hearted motions to connect just won't do. You're doing the relationship hokey pokey, putting one foot in and then putting one foot out and shaking yourself all about into a frenzy. You need more quality time from this person, but they're just mirroring your own behavior...in one day and done the next. No one's a mind-reader, not even you. An old love may look tempting now, but it's more likely to be a temporary boost to your ego. Figure out the relationship dynamic in front of you, and what you're willing to consistently invest to make it work.

PISCES: Venus retrogrades in your sixth house of work and well-being. Your heart may be wondering if "eating your feelings" is really doing anything for your well-being (you know it probably isn't, but you're an expert at rationalizing your indulgences). There's something you're unwilling to face about changes you need to make so you can feel more like yourself on the daily. You could be dealing with a "frenemy" at your workplace and their false front could be particularly galling now. Or maybe a work place romance (ill-advised, but too late to apologize now) goes sour or feeds the office gossip mill. Don't take other people's shenanigans out on yourself. Recalibrate through self-care rituals—journaling can help you decide what you need to do to take care of yourself in this situation. If you feel a job change is in order, wait until after the retrograde is over to make that decision; often situations clear up naturally after a planet goes direct again.

11

Monthly Horoscopes and "Lucky Days"

MAKE YOUR LIFE EASIER and luckier by working with the astrological energies, instead of against them. You can reference the "lucky days" not only for your Sun Sign, but also for your Moon and Rising Signs.

To determine the most beneficial days, I used an ephemeris based in eastern time, United States, being careful to avoid the "void of course" moon periods when the moon does not make any aspects with other planets. Aspects (interactions) are what create the astrological influences. No influence, no result.

If you don't know your Moon and Rising signs, you can go to Astro.com and get a free birth chart. You'll need your day, time, and place of birth to determine your Rising Sign and Moon Sign. Also, if you are born on the cusp, time and place are crucial in determining if you are indeed one sign or the other. (You can be born on June 21st, for example, and still be a Gemini, with your Sun at 29 degrees 52 minutes and 28 seconds. But you would definitely be a Gemini, and not a Cancer.)

Lucky Days for your Sun Sign: Work on important goals; let yourself shine; push yourself out of a comfort zone. Enjoy romantic and creative activities.

Lucky Days for your Moon Sign: Tend to home, family, garden, pets, your emotional needs. Good for self-care, journaling, home-cooked meals, time with friends, escape from the daily grind. Relax.

Lucky Days for your Rising Sign: Show up in the world! Give a presentation, attend important meetings, interview for that job, go on a first date, take care of your physical body (personal grooming, clothes shopping, etc.)

It's important to remember that the Stars suggest, but do not compel. While certain days may have a more flowing and favorable vibe, results still depend upon your own awareness, alignment, and actions.

For each month I've provided a brief highlight of certain planetary movements you may want to bear in mind, including analysis of the new and full moons. Following that are your suggested Lucky Days for all twelve Zodiac signs.

JANUARY

**Mars is still retrograde in Gemini until January 12; Mercury is retrograde in Capricorn until January 18. ** As such, use the good luck days before January 18 for revisiting a situation, project etc. that's already been in the works. See the earlier chapter on Mercury retrograde for specific advice.

The full moon in Cancer on the sixth could bring up some tender feelings from the past as Mercury retrograde squares Chiron the Wounded Healer in Aries. Moon energy relates to cycles, so you could gain clarity on a repetitive situation that isn't the best for you. This full moon can give you the emotional insight into how you may not always make decisions in your best interests and end up regretting it. Now, you can see how to break this pattern and heal a long-standing issue. Be compassionate with yourself as you come to terms with making an important change in your life. The full moon in Cancer is an opportune time to practice self-care, renew your relationships, and reconnect with your inner self.

On January 21, the new moon in Aquarius lifts the mood. Gong Hee Fot Choy! ... and just like that, it's the Year of the Rabbit and we're free at least from the delays of the retrogrades earlier in the month. Jupiter in Aries and Mars in Gemini are in favorable alignment to this new moon, so put your big, bold (Jupiter) action plan (Mars) into writing (Gemini) and envision your future (Aquarius). While vision boards can be great (I love them myself), putting your intentions down in paper, in your own handwriting, is more beneficial in manifesting with this new moon.

ARIES Lucky Stars: 8, 9, 12, 25, 26
TAURUS Lucky Stars: 20, 27, 28, 29
GEMINI Lucky Stars: 3, 12, 18, 22, 30, 31
CANCER Lucky Stars: 6, 15, 16, 26
LEO Lucky Stars: 8, 9, 26, 30, 31
VIRGO Lucky Stars: 11, 20, 28, 29
LIBRA Lucky Stars: 13, 14, 22, 26, 30, 31
SCORPIO Lucky Stars: 6, 15, 16, 24, 26, 31
SAGITTARIUS Lucky Stars: 6, 8, 18, 22, 26
CAPRICORN Lucky Stars: 11, 20, 22, 28, 29
AQUARIUS Lucky Stars: 20, 22, 30, 31
PISCES Lucky Stars: 6, 15, 16, 26, 28, 29

FEBRUARY

The full moon in Leo on the fifth is a bit of a powder keg, with the moon in a tense alignment with Uranus in Taurus. Mars in Gemini is squaring Venus in Pisces, so full moon fights could center around power dynamics in relationships. The sparks could fly—literally, figuratively. (Make up sex? Maybe...).

The new moon in Pisces on February 20 happens at one degree, and is also the same day Venus enters Aries, which has us fired up and motivated to *get on with it, already.* As you set your intentions at the Pisces new moon on the twentieth, keep in mind that Saturn is getting ready to soon activate this new moon degree when he enters Pisces on March 7; Saturn in Pisces will encourage us to work with inspired discipline toward making our dreams a reality. See more on the Saturn and Neptune in Pisces chapter earlier in this book.

ARIES Lucky Stars: 12, 14, 20, 22, 23
TAURUS Lucky Stars: 7, 8, 21, 24, 25
GEMINI Lucky Stars: 9, 10, 14, 27
CANCER Lucky Stars: 2, 3, 7, 20, 21
LEO Lucky Stars: 14, 20, 22, 23, 27
VIRGO Lucky Stars: 7, 8, 21, 24, 25
LIBRA Lucky Stars: 4, 5, 9, 10, 27
SCORPIO Lucky Stars: 7, 12, 20, 21, 25
SAGITTARIUS Lucky Stars: 14, 22, 23, 27
CAPRICORN Lucky Stars: 7, 8, 16, 18, 21
AQUARIUS Lucky Stars: 7, 10, 18, 27
PISCES Lucky Stars: 2, 12, 18, 20, 21

MARCH

March starts with Venus conjunct Jupiter on the second/third (depending on time zone), roaring in with Aries exuberance to push your luck. The full moon in Virgo on March 7 is the same day Saturn approaches the Aquarian finish line of 29 degrees, ready to enter Pisces. Try not to give in to the Virgo tendency to worry and over-analyze during this time of transition. Multiple chapters are finishing up now.

Set your sights on the new moon in Aries on March 21st, at 0 degrees 48 minutes...this new moon is a significant symbol of this year's energy of regeneration. We are literally starting over with hope and enthusiasm in the Aries sector of our charts at the true beginning of the new year: the spring equinox. Two days after the new moon, Pluto enters Aquarius, and the energetic shift is palpable. See the chapter earlier in this book for greater insight into how Pluto in Aquarius will influence your life.

ARIES Lucky Stars: 2, 3, 19, 22, 28, 31
TAURUS Lucky Stars: 6, 15, 16, 24, 30
GEMINI Lucky Stars: 9, 18, 19, 26
CANCER Lucky Stars: 2, 12, 25, 29, 30
LEO Lucky Stars: 2, 3, 22, 26, 28, 31
VIRGO Lucky Stars: 6, 7, 15, 16, 30
LIBRA Lucky Stars: 9, 14, 18, 23, 30
SCORPIO Lucky Stars: 6, 11, 12, 24, 30
SAGITTARIUS Lucky Stars: 2, 3, 13, 14, 22, 26, 28
CAPRICORN Lucky Stars: 6, 7, 15, 16, 23, 24, 30
AQUARIUS Lucky Stars: 4, 9, 18, 23
PISCES Lucky Stars: 6, 12, 25, 28, 29, 30

APRIL

On April 6, the full moon in Libra opposes Chiron, illuminating what has healed and what has not regarding boundaries and balance in relationships. The Aries vibe is strong this month, as the Sun conjuncts lucky Jupiter on April 11, the same day Venus enters Gemini and trines Pluto in Aquarius. Life-changing conversations regarding love and/or money are in the frame.

The second new moon (total solar eclipse) in Aries season occurs on April 20, at 29 degrees, considered a "critical" degree in astrology. Sometimes referred to as "the degree of fate," 29 degrees represents a cycle coming to a close. So it's ironic that we are having a new moon solar eclipse in this degree, in the sign of Aries, which represents beginnings. There is likely some unfinished business you need to take care of before you can proceed into the next powerful chapter of your life, which as I wrote about in the Nodal Shift chapter, begins when the North Node enters Aries on July 17/18 (depending on time zone), triggering the degree of this eclipse at that time.

You may not be able to fully immerse yourself in the seed planting stage of this solar eclipse until you first prepare the ground—by wrapping up loose ends, completing a project, relationship, situation that could have its roots in late 2004/early 2005 or during the transit of Uranus through Aries (mentioned in my North Node chapter).

During a solar eclipse, the light of the life-giving Sun is temporarily obscured, a cosmic invitation to look into the deeper recesses of your life, as a sort of spiritual reset. Since you're going to be on a whole new "destined" mission starting in mid-July, it is advisable at this eclipse to reflect on how our Spirit is doing vis-à-vis joy, creativity, love, light, generosity, innovation, and daring—the good vibrations that come from the Sun in Aries—in whatever house Aries rules in your natal chart.

Good news can often arrive at a solar eclipse; at this critical 29 degree, that news may involve a surprise as Mercury and Uranus will be conjunct in Taurus. Mars will be in Cancer, the sign of its "fall"—meaning that Mars' usual assertive nature is weakened. Mars is the ruler of Aries (sign of the eclipse), so this is significant. Chiron in Aries squares Mars, bringing pressure to change our typical emotional responses. Jupiter's also in Aries, trying to guide you to see the higher purpose of whatever is going down and not to get stuck in passive/aggressive tendencies, if the surprise temporarily disrupts you. In my view, there's a real "blessing in disguise" vibe to this eclipse, an opportunity to release old and stuck emotional energy through the psychic purge of a sob session (good use of Mars in Cancer), and an acceptance that *the end is where you start from* (to paraphrase T.S. Eliot).

The day after the eclipse, Mercury goes retrograde in Taurus, so review your finances and commitments of time and energy, and make adjustments as necessary so that you have what you need to move forward on your dreams in the remainder of 2023.

ARIES Lucky Stars: 10, 11, 18, 19
TAURUS Lucky Stars: 2, 3, 16, 30
GEMINI Lucky Stars: 5, 11, 14, 23
CANCER Lucky Stars: 8, 16, 25
LEO Lucky Stars: 1, 10, 11, 28
VIRGO Lucky Stars: 3, 11, 12, 30
LIBRA Lucky Stars: 5, 14, 27, 28
SCORPIO Lucky Stars: 7, 8, 12, 16, 30
SAGITTARIUS Lucky Stars: 1, 5, 10, 11, 28
CAPRICORN Lucky Stars: 8, 11, 12, 14, 30
AQUARIUS Lucky Stars: 5, 10, 14, 23
PISCES Lucky Stars: 11, 12, 16, 25

MAY

** Pluto goes retrograde on May 1; Mercury is retrograde in Taurus until the fifteenth. **

There's one more full moon lunar eclipse in Scorpio to contend with until 2032, in nearly the same degree as the full moon lunar eclipse in Taurus back on November 8, 2022. This time the moon is opposite rather than conjunct surprise-a-minute Uranus. Look back to November 2022 for clues on how this cycle might wrap up for you, especially since Mercury is retrograde at this time (classic indication of previous situations returning for move-along closure). Mars is in Cancer, trining the moon, so you'll have the emotional intelligence to act on your best interests, despite whatever ghost from your past may haunt you.

Jupiter enters Taurus on May 16. Three days later, the new moon in Taurus sends kisses to Neptune in Pisces, perfect for manifesting sublime romance and poetry. Mars enters Leo on May 20, and spring fever is a glorious vibe—indulge yourself in a fanciful pursuit.

ARIES Lucky Stars: 5, 16, 20
TAURUS Lucky Stars: 16, 18, 28
GEMINI Lucky Stars: 5, 20, 25
CANCER Lucky Stars: 7, 22, 23
LEO Lucky Stars: 20, 25, 30
VIRGO Lucky Stars: 16, 27, 28
LIBRA Lucky Stars: 2, 7, 21, 30
SCORPIO Lucky Stars: 13, 16, 22
SAGITTARIUS Lucky Stars: 7, 15, 20
CAPRICORN Lucky Stars: 9, 16, 27
AQUARIUS Lucky Stars: 3, 11, 30
PISCES Lucky Stars: 13, 16, 22

JUNE

The full moon in Sagittarius on June 4 trines Chiron in Aries and Mars in Leo, illuminating a hopeful and healing truth about your own brave heart and how wise you've been to follow it.

On the June 11, Pluto backtracks into Capricorn, and it's time to write the last few lines of a long story that began with Pluto's entry into Capricorn in 2008. Saturn retrogrades in Pisces on June 17, encouraging review of commitments and whether or not expectations are realistic.

The new moon in Gemini on the June 18 faces Neptune in Pisces throwing some shade on its parade. It's time to be realistic about what you can do now and what may need to be postponed for another time. Neptune retrogrades June 30, and you turn inward to piece together the last bits of a karmic puzzle.

ARIES Lucky Stars: 5, 6, 12
TAURUS Lucky Stars: 4, 14, 24
GEMINI Lucky Stars: 4, 16, 17, 27
CANCER Lucky Stars: 1, 26, 27, 29
LEO Lucky Stars: 5, 6, 12, 17
VIRGO Lucky Stars: 4, 14, 19
LIBRA Lucky Stars: 4, 5, 27
SCORPIO Lucky Stars: 1, 10, 29
SAGITTARIUS Lucky Stars: 4, 6, 12
CAPRICORN Lucky Stars: 4, 6, 24
AQUARIUS Lucky Stars: 8, 16, 27
PISCES Lucky Stars: 2, 10, 19

JULY

The full moon in Capricorn on July 3 is intense—Uranus in Taurus causes friction for Mars and Venus in Leo, and Mercury conjunct the Sun in Cancer rides the waves of some deep emotional processing—perhaps due to a surprise revelation. Uranus in Taurus is on Capricorn's side here, so whatever may be revealed is designed to help you take charge of the situation. Capricorn hates to play games, so if news arrives of a love triangle or some other sort of shenanigan (someone using flattery to gain an unfair business advantage or manipulating a situation to suit their own greedy agenda), then Capricorn will not hesitate to cut the connection cold.

On July 12, the North Node enters Aries. On July 17, the new moon in Cancer squares the North Node in Aries, which is square Pluto retrograde in Capricorn (opposite this new moon). The past may still tug at your heartstrings, but if you want a new beginning, it's really time to let it go. It's time to blaze a new trail for yourself, which leads you to a new home, new workplace, new way of life.

Venus retrogrades in Leo on July 23. See separate chapter earlier in this book on what you need to know about this transit.

ARIES Lucky Stars: 9, 12, 18
TAURUS Lucky Stars: 3, 12, 21
GEMINI Lucky Stars: 13, 14, 24, 29
CANCER Lucky Stars: 3, 7, 16, 21
LEO Lucky Stars: 1, 11, 19
VIRGO Lucky Stars: 11, 21, 28, 29
LIBRA Lucky Stars: 5, 14, 24
SCORPIO Lucky Stars: 7, 16, 26
SAGITTARIUS Lucky Stars: 1, 9, 24, 28
CAPRICORN Lucky Stars: 3, 12, 21, 29, 30
AQUARIUS Lucky Stars: 5, 11, 28
PISCES Lucky Stars: 3, 7, 26

AUGUST

August is one of the trickiest months in 2023.

** Venus is retrograde in Leo the entire month.**

Mercury goes retrograde on August 23, in Virgo, the same day the Sun enters Virgo. (*Special note to Virgos:* you will have Mercury retrograde in your solar return for your birthday year ahead. You may be doing a lot of "soul searching," and it's time to clear up what is already on your to-do list rather than piling more on. Since Mercury is your ruling planet, this retrograde is especially impactful, and it may help you redefine yourself in important ways, especially in terms of when and how much you're willing to do for other people, and what you need from your job in order to be happy.)

Two full moons bookend the month: one on the first in Aquarius, square Jupiter in Taurus, and the other on August 31, in Pisces, conjunct

Saturn. Sandwiched in between is a new moon in Leo on the sixteenth conjunct retrograde Venus but exactly in tense alignment with Uranus in Taurus.

There is a distinct one step forward, two steps back vibe this month. You may second guess yourself at the first full moon, perhaps trying to emotionally dial down a tense situation involving love or money that has its roots in the past. At the new moon, someone may promise to turn over a new leaf (and that someone could be you!); however, with Venus retrograde, the promises are not worth the gold-flecked, rose-scented paper they're written on.

Mars enters Libra on the August 27, putting the focus on our relationships (which have probably already been going through challenging re-adjustments this month). Mars is a planet of action (often without much forethought); Libra likes to think before acting—this can be a frustrating combination, considering all the other prevailing energies this month. Then the blue Pisces moon faces a stern "I-told-you-so" wagging finger from retrograde Saturn on the thirty-first, and you're rethinking everything (thanks, Mercury retrograde) that you thought had already been decided.

Uranus goes retrograde on the August 29.

ARIES Lucky Stars: 5, 6, 15, 25
TAURUS Lucky Stars: 3, 8, 18, 30
GEMINI Lucky Stars: 1, 10, 18, 25, 27
CANCER Lucky Stars: 12, 13, 30, 31
LEO Lucky Stars: 15, 18, 24, 25
VIRGO Lucky Stars: 7, 8, 18, 27, 28
LIBRA Lucky Stars: 1, 10, 15, 20, 27
SCORPIO Lucky Stars: 3, 17, 30, 31
SAGITTARIUS Lucky Stars: 6, 9, 15, 20, 25, 27
CAPRICORN Lucky Stars: 8, 27, 30, 31
AQUARIUS Lucky Stars: 1, 10, 20, 29
PISCES Lucky Stars: 3, 12, 13, 23

SEPTEMBER

Jupiter retrogrades in Taurus on September 4.

Venus is retrograde in Leo until the September 4.

Mercury is retrograde in Virgo until September 15.

The new moon in Virgo on September 15 awakens you to the practical steps you can take to make your love, money, and creative dreams moving forward again now that Venus and Mercury are direct. (Granted, Jupiter, Saturn, Uranus, Neptune, and Pluto are all retrograde, but their influence tends more to the larger themes of our lives. Mercury and Venus are more influential when it comes to daily influence, so having them both go direct again is welcome news, indeed!).

On September 29, the full moon in Aries highlights the "me/we" axis of self and others, just as Libra's ruler Venus (transiting Leo) squares Uranus in Taurus. Sudden revelations about someone's true feelings—for better or worse—are divulged. Will you be going it alone or have the urge to merge based on what you discover? Pluto retrograding in Capricorn squaring the south node in Libra suggests whatever happens is karmic in nature.

ARIES Lucky Stars: 2, 11, 21, 29
TAURUS Lucky Stars: 4, 14, 16, 21
GEMINI Lucky Stars: 6, 13, 16, 23
CANCER Lucky Stars: 8, 9, 15, 24
LEO Lucky Stars: 11, 15, 20, 29
VIRGO Lucky Stars: 13, 14, 16, 18
LIBRA Lucky Stars: 4, 6, 16, 25
SCORPIO Lucky Stars: 9, 18, 19, 20, 27
SAGITTARIUS Lucky Stars: 2, 15, 27, 29
CAPRICORN Lucky Stars: 3, 15, 18, 23, 24

AQUARIUS Lucky Stars: 6, 15, 25, 30
PISCES Lucky Stars: 8, 9, 24, 27

OCTOBER

Pluto goes direct on October 10 - Capricorns born in the last few days of Capricorn, take note. We will all feel this energy, but people born during that time are especially empowered to work with Pluto's regenerative influence and rise like the phoenix from the ashes of the old.

On October 14, the new moon solar eclipse in Libra is conjunct Mercury, and the North Node in Aries is square Pluto (now direct) in Capricorn. You may be of two minds on how to proceed with a new direction in your life; or perhaps feel as though you have one foot in the new, and one still in the old. Rash moves are not advised; proceed systematically, but proceed nevertheless.

The full moon eclipse in Taurus on October 28 is in a wide conjunction to Jupiter and opposes a Mercury/Mars conjunction in Scorpio. Jupiter in Taurus may exaggerate a stubborn attitude—yours or someone else's. And in this battle of wills, words can be weaponized under the Mercury/Mars transit; be careful to whom you direct such potent energy, especially on a lunar eclipse when endings are a distinct possibility.

ARIES Lucky Stars: 9, 12, 18, 27
TAURUS Lucky Stars: 1, 11, 12, 22, 29
GEMINI Lucky Stars: 4, 14, 20, 31
CANCER Lucky Stars: 6, 16, 20, 24, 25
LEO Lucky Stars: 3, 9, 18, 27
VIRGO Lucky Stars: 3, 11, 13, 20
LIBRA Lucky Stars: 4, 13, 14, 22, 31
SCORPIO Lucky Stars: 11, 13, 16, 22, 24, 25

SAGITTARIUS Lucky Stars: 9, 18, 20, 27
CAPRICORN Lucky Stars: 11, 22, 24, 20
AQUARIUS Lucky Stars: 3, 4, 21, 25, 31
PISCES Lucky Stars: 6, 16, 21, 24, 25

NOVEMBER

On November 4, Saturn goes direct.

The November 13 new moon in Scorpio is conjunct Mars, trine Neptune in Pisces, and opposite Uranus retrograde in Taurus. Back in the day, Mars was the ruler of Scorpio, and thus Mars is comfortable here; Mars in Scorpio directs his arrow of desire with striking surgical precision. Conjunct the new moon, Mars brings the emotional heat to the Scorpio area of your chart; trining Neptune, he cuts through the fog of denial and delay, and opposing Uranus, he issues an emotional ultimatum of "now or never" that could rock your and/or someone else's world. This is an intense moon that propels you off the fence to take action, stat!

Mars is in the frame again on November 27 when the full moon in Gemini opposes Mars newly arrived on Sagittarius's doorstep. Mercury, Gemini's ruler, is in Sadge, squaring Neptune...and with Mars conjunct the Sun, ego tripping comes to mind. Truth telling Mercury in Sagittarius may rain on someone's parade (Neptune in Pisces) or flat out expose some serious porkies (or "fibonaccis" as I like to call them). If someone has been creative with the truth, that can definitely be exposed now, but whomever is doing the exposing needs to keep an eye on their smugness at doing so—as all the facts might not be revealed—or it could be discovered later that what was perceived as a lie was actually an honest omission or misunderstanding or use of "creative" license. In other words, someone's need to call someone out may be overblown, considering what they are calling the person out on. Mountains out of molehills and all that.

ARIES Lucky Stars: 14, 17, 23, 24
TAURUS Lucky Stars: 7, 8, 15, 16, 17
GEMINI Lucky Stars: 4, 8, 10, 15, 27
CANCER Lucky Stars: 2, 3, 12, 13, 27, 30
LEO Lucky Stars: 5, 7, 14, 17, 23
VIRGO Lucky Stars: 4, 8, 10, 17
LIBRA Lucky Stars: 8, 10, 18, 19, 27
SCORPIO Lucky Stars: 2, 8, 12, 13, 21
SAGITTARIUS Lucky Stars: 10, 14, 16, 23
CAPRICORN Lucky Stars: 4, 7, 16, 17, 29
AQUARIUS Lucky Stars: 4, 8, 14, 19, 27
PISCES Lucky Stars: 2, 3, 17, 29

DECEMBER

Neptune goes direct on December 6.

On December 13, Mercury goes retrograde in Capricorn.

The new moon in Sagittarius on December 12 trines the North Node in Aries, a beautiful energy of setting intentions to take action on the new doors opening for you in this area of your chart (see previous chapter on the Nodal Shift). A trine is characterized by effortless flow, so you could find that a plan is coming together easily.

December 27 features another lovely trine, this time between the full moon in Cancer and Saturn (now direct) in Pisces. You have the maturity to take emotional responsibility for yourself and your choices, and this full moon could affirm what is working well in that regard and what may still need a few tweaks. Commitments made now are serious; those involved are "playing for keeps."

On December 31, Jupiter resumes direct motion in Taurus, resuming the generous flow of gifts and goodies into our lives.

ARIES Lucky Stars: 2, 12, 16, 20, 31
TAURUS Lucky Stars: 5, 22, 27, 30
GEMINI Lucky Stars: 2, 3, 7, 11, 16, 25
CANCER Lucky Stars: 4, 14, 18, 22, 27
LEO Lucky Stars: 2, 7, 22, 29, 30
VIRGO Lucky Stars: 5, 7, 11, 14, 18
LIBRA Lucky Stars: 4, 7, 22, 23, 25
SCORPIO Lucky Stars: 4, 18, 24, 27
SAGITTARIUS Lucky Stars: 11, 12, 20, 29, 30
CAPRICORN Lucky Stars: 5, 9, 14, 22, 24
AQUARIUS Lucky Stars: 5, 7, 19, 25, 29
PISCES Lucky Stars: 18, 23, 25, 27, 31

12

Year Ahead Horoscope Summary & Affirmations

ARIES: This is your year to feel like your exuberant self again—wild, fierce, free—doing your thing and loving life with your unstoppable fire. In many ways, Aries, you're just getting started on the next 20 year chapter of your life. While you may have many opportunities to choose from, especially in March/April, be discerning and select with care, considering the longer-term implication of your choices. Mid-December could bring a significant new connection (business or personal) with an international flair.

Affirmations for Aries in 2023:
I am capable of achieving my most cherished dreams.
I am strong and confident in who I am and I lead with authenticity.
I welcome new experiences and opportunities that help me grow into the next chapter of my life
I am filled with gratitude for my increasing prosperity.
I am in control of my own destiny.

TAURUS: The year ahead continues to revolutionize your life, Taurus, and although at times you are simply in jaw-dropping awe of the changes—wondering if you can handle them (you can)—a part of you knows that this shake-up is exactly what you need. Mid to end of May could be an especially joyful time for you. A gorgeous wish could manifest for you around the new moon in Virgo in mid-September. Changes could rock your world at the beginning of November—keep calm and carry on!

Affirmations for Taurus in 2023:
I am manifesting abundance in all areas of my life.
I am happy with the life I am choosing to create.
I handle changes and challenges with grace and poise.
I am worthy of receiving love and respect from others.
I am grounded and focused on achieving my desires.

GEMINI: In the next twelve months, many of your aspirations can be realized—some through simple hard work and others through the serendipity of the Universe putting you in the right place at the right time. The first three weeks of April can be magical, Gemini, for your love life and creative projects. The eclipse in mid-October is especially potent, helping you heal a karmic situation and move onto a new chapter.

Affirmations for Gemini in 2023:
I am creative and open to new ideas and perspectives.
I am ready to manifest the next level of success in my career.
I am confident in my abilities and in my decision-making.
I pay attention to the signs from the Universe.
I am surrounded by positivity and joy.

CANCER: The year ahead promises resolution with pesky relationship issues. And although loving connections are never far from your mind, Cancer, this year you're focusing more on your personal ambitions. Travel is beneficial for you in so many ways, but especially in terms of fueling the expansive feeling that *the world is your oyster*. Mid to end of May is ideal for a fantastic voyage. You're releasing yourself from a karmic tie at the beginning of July; it's time.

Affirmations for Cancer in 2023:
I deepen my connection to my intuition and listen to its directives.
I am worthy of abundance and recognition.
I am capable of achieving my greatest ambitions.
I lovingly release myself from karmic contracts.
I explore my world with curiosity and joy.

LEO: This is your year to live large, Leo, and expand your world through travel, international connections, writing/study, and through taking advantage of a lucky break that's finally arriving in your career zone. Travel far afield is supported by the stars the first three weeks of April. Your career is likely to become quite busy from mid-May onward. Watch any tendency to doubt yourself in August. Mid to end of September may see fresh opportunities to improve your finances (connected with career betterment).

Affirmations for Leo in 2023:
I am passionately and courageously creating a new life for myself.
I am confident in using my own Power for good.
I am manifesting better and more aligned career opportunities.
I welcome joyful connections into my life.
I am a rising Star.

VIRGO: The next twelve months you are in the perfect position, Virgo, to manifest valuable resources, connections, mentors, and relationships that improve your life in every way. It is imperative to release any blocks/limiting beliefs/baggage/relationships that stand in the way of actualizing your highest potential. The first three weeks of March help you ascertain who/what needs to go or can stay. Settle important career matters at the end of June. In mid-September, you are moving forward confidently with new plans!

Affirmations for Virgo in 2023:
I am worthy of all the good things Life has to offer.
I trust in myself completely and know that I can do anything when I apply myself.
I deserve, manifest, and invest in relationships that are good for me.

I explore new career opportunities that showcase my talents.
I am calm and confident that I am doing what is best for me.

LIBRA: In the year ahead you are making important decisions concerning your relationships (both business and personal). Imbalances in power dynamics must be addressed, Libra; you do yourself no favors by holding onto dead-end situations that simply continue to drain you. The first three weeks of April show you "who loves ya, baby"—from mid-July onward, the energies favor deepening worthy personal associations. A connection from your past could resurface mid-October in order to wrap up a karmic contract.

Affirmations for Libra in 2023:
I attract caring connections into my life.
I am surrounded by love and kindness.
I am resilient and open to new experiences.
I choose to be happy.
I free myself from unhealthy attachments that disturb my inner peace.

SCORPIO: Over the next year, Scorpio, you are committing to new personal projects that could bring in a fresh revenue stream. You're also getting out of the house more—meeting, greeting, socializing—and possibly finding the Love of Your Life. Mid-May to mid-July is especially favorable for forging new connections. The new moon in your sign on November 13th skyrockets your motivation and you take action on an important decision that could change the trajectory of your life rather dramatically.

Affirmations for Scorpio in 2023:
I accept and love myself for who I am.
I am open to new relationships that enhance my Life and appreciate my energy.
I am confidently creative.
I am grateful for prosperity that flows to me from many sources and many directions.
I am willing to change.

SAGITTARIUS: The year ahead rejuvenates your Spirit in so many ways, Sagittarius, particularly from the end of January to the end of April. Life hasn't felt this good in a long time—and you are grateful for every new creative idea, loving connection, and pleasurable experience. A decision you made in December 2022 to take a leap of faith could pay off handsomely for you the first three weeks of April. A heartfelt wish could come true for you mid-December 2023, and you will be amazed at the positive ways your life has changed in only one short year.

Affirmations for Sagittarius in 2023:
I am grateful for all the good things in my Life.
I am abundance personified.
I am creative and wise in my thinking.
I am selective about who and what I give my Life force energy to.
I travel beyond any preconceived notions of what I am capable of and surprise myself in what I can accomplish when I focus.

CAPRICORN: This is your year, Capricorn, to regenerate your world from the ground up. You're finding your place in the Sun—and even if this doesn't involve a physical move to a more aligned town—you are feeling more at home in the world than you have in ages. No one can take away the resilient strength of spirit you've cultivated over the last fifteen years. You've more than earned the happiness that 2023 would like to bring to your door. Set your prosperity plans in motion after the new moon in Aquarius on January 21. Mid to end of May, enjoy a trip for business and/or pleasure. Mid-October, questions about a new career path/project are answered.

Affirmations for Capricorn in 2023:
I am empowered to reach my highest potential.
I welcome with open arms all the happiness the Universe has to offer me.
I trust in the power of my creative genius to manifest new revenue streams.
I am healthy, wealthy, wise, and well-loved.
I am successful beyond my wildest dreams.

AQUARIUS: This year will feel lighter, Aquarius, as Saturn finally leaves your sign at the beginning of March. The karmic tests you've passed over the last three years have taught you valuable lessons in boundaries, truth-telling, and commitments. Your daily life undergoes vast improvements—through better communication, healed relationships with family/siblings/friends, and beneficial changes in your home environment. In April you have "the gift of the gab" and could catch a lucky break because of it. Mid-December fires up your creative juices and you start a project that "monetizes your mind"—which could bring great rewards after Jupiter moves into Gemini on May 25, 2024.

Affirmations for Aquarius in 2023:
I am strong and confident and have unwavering trust in my intuition.
I am a creative genius.
I speak my truth with a loving heart.
I surround myself with energies, people, situations that support my well-being.
I am focused on making my home a healing sanctuary.

PISCES: Over the ensuing twelve months, you are entering a phase of great personal empowerment, Pisces. Through a renewed commitment to your personal values, you increase your prosperity, especially from end of January through mid-April. A sweetheart deal could happen for you the first week of March or between April 3 and 13. Sell yourself and your ideas, especially between mid-May and mid-July. In December 2023, you may find yourself breaking new ground in your career; others can't get enough of your energy and expertise!

Affirmations for Pisces in 2023:
I am clear on my priorities, values, and boundaries.
I am inspired to explore my creative potential.
I invest in my artistry and create what is important to me.
I welcome greater prosperity into my life and I manage this bounty wisely.
I organize my life so that I have more time for who/what matters to me.

About Stella Wilde

Stella is a cosmic pathfinder, intuitive advisor, and manifestation mentor. You can find her at https://stellawilde.com

Catch up with her on the socials for astro alerts, tarot truths, and manifestation magic.

- youtube.com/@StellaWilde
- facebook.com/realstellawilde
- instagram.com/realstellawilde
- pinterest.com/stellawilde0038
- twitter.com/realstellawilde

Made in United States
Orlando, FL
08 February 2023